DOORWAY TO HELL

Disaster in Somalia

Brig. General Ed Wheeler (USA-Ret)
&
Lt. Colonel Craig Roberts (USA-Ret)

FRONTLINE BOOKS, LONDON

Doorway to Hell: Disaster in Somalia
This edition published in 2012 by Frontline Books

an imprint of Pen & Sword Books Ltd,
47 Church Street, Barnsley, S. Yorkshire, S70 2AS
www.frontline-books.com

ISBN: 978-1-84832-680-4

CIP data records for this title are available from the British Library

For more information on our books, please visit
www.frontline-books.com, email info@frontline-books.com
or write to us at the above address.

Printed and bound by CPI Group (UK) Ltd, Croydon, CR0 4YY

Books by Craig Roberts

The Medusa File: Crimes and Coverups of the U.S. Government (CPI, 1997)

Kill Zone: A Sniper Looks at Dealey Plaza (CPI, 1994)

JFK: The Dead Witnesses (CPI, 1995) (With John Armstrong)

Police Sniper (Pocket Books, 1993)

Combat Medic–Vietnam (Pocket Books, 1991)

The Walking Dead: A Marine's Story of Vietnam (Pocket Books, 1989) (co-authored with Charles W. Sasser)

One Shot–One Kill: America's Combat Snipers (Pocket Books, 1990) (co-authored with Charles W. Sasser).

Hellhound (Avon, 1994, Fiction) (co-authored with Allen Appel III and Allen Appel IV)

ACKNOWLEDGEMENTS

The research and preparation of this narrative would not have been possible without the guidance, assistance, direction, and contributions of Professor Thomas Buckley, University of Tulsa History Department.

On behalf of his soldiers' families and loved ones, I wish to extend my personal appreciation to a lengthy list of U.S. Marines , Air Force and Navy personnel as well as State and Defense Department officials. However, specifically special appreciation is extended to U.S. Army Lieutenant Colonel Robert L. Davis, the last commander of the 43rd Engineer Combat Battalion (Heavy), during both Operations Restore and Continue Hope. He led a total of over a thousand troops through the "doorway to hell" twice, and brought them all back alive. Special acknowledgment is also extended to Major Mark Feierstein, 36th Engineer Group S-4 (Logistics) during Operation Restore Hope and 43rd S-3 (Operations) during Operation Continue Hope; Major Alan Estes, 43rd S-3 (Operations) during Operation Restore Hope; Captain Brian Unwin, Surgeon, 43rd Engineer Combat Battalion (H) during Operation Restore Hope; Captain Dale Forrester, 43rd Chaplain, Operation Restore Hope; Captain Jeffrey T. Bochonok, 43rd S-1 (Personnel/Admin) during Operation Continue Hope; First Lieutenant Brian E. Wheeler, the 43rd's Signal Officer and Command Sergeant Major Lawrence Maxwell, both of whom served during Operations Restore Hope and Continue Hope; and Sergeant Hans Smith, 43rd Operations NCO who served during the Somalian Aid Mission in 1985, and during Operation Continue Hope. These men, who were based at Fort Benning, Georgia and deployed to Somalia with their colleagues of the 43rd Engineers, served unselfishly and heroically. In doing so, twice they walked through the "Doorway to Hell" for a nation that ultimately wished they hadn't gone at all.

It would not have been possible to include as rich a variety of source material without the support and assistance of my mother, Mrs. Eleanore S. Wheeler, Ormond Beach, Florida, who first saw the United States Military Academy at West Point, New York in 1915. Seventy-five years later she returned a second time to see her grandson graduate in 1990.

I extend my special appreciation to my wife Marcia Jane Largen Wheeler, who provided invaluable service in the initial editing of this material and is representative of the mothers who supplied the servicemen and women who fought--and died -- in a land few Americans could find on a map of the world.

Allied perspectives were also provided through the contributions of British Army Sergeant Terry W. Young, London Regiment (Territorial), formerly the 6/7 Queens (Territorial) Regiment, British Army (Retired).

Finally, this work is dedicated to the forty-three American Soldiers and Marines and two civilians who were killed in Somalia, East Africa, during Operations Restore Hope and Continue Hope, between December 9, 1992 and March 25, 1994. They have joined other Americans over whom, as Captain John D. McRae so eloquently wrote in his poem *In Flanders Fields*, "the poppies blow / between the crosses, row on row."

BG Ed Wheeler, USA (Ret)

Doorway to Hell

In memory of my mother and wife, both of whom lived just long enough to see our son return from Somalia and harm's way .... twice.

FOREWORD

Despite an undeniable desperate need for help by numerous other countries throughout Africa, Operation Restore Hope was initiated in Somalia, East Africa in December, 1992 by the United Nations. The mission of the intervention, led by the United States, was--according to official sources--to save the Somalian people from starvation.

Tactically, Operation Restore Hope was a success. By the spring of 1993, most of Somalia--outside of the capital city of Mogadishu-- was secured. Protected by U.S. and allied combat forces, American army engineers, fulfilling their assigned mission checklist, rebuilt the Somalian road network to permit the distribution of food supplies to rural areas. Due to this humanitarian rescue mission, tens of thousands of Somalians were saved from dying of starvation and resultant diseases brought about by malnutrition, and other conditions resulting from civil war and the lack of sanitation.

Had the intervention ended then, it would have represented a shining example of what mankind was capable of doing when nations worked together. Unfortunately, what might have been recorded as a victory of historical proportions for the nations which united behind the effort to save the Somalian people, deteriorated into an ignoble and humiliating defeat for the United Nations.

Why did the intervention in a fourth-world African country, supported by the United Nations and backed by the leading industrialized nations of the world, deteriorate from a classic humanitarian achievement to a world-class disaster in a matter of months?

Why did an American administration--and Congress--allow American forces to be committed to an open-ended mission of "nation building" under the auspices and direction of the United Nations, which was an entirely different mission than that of saving the Somalian people from starvation?

Were there other hidden reasons for international intervention in Somalia that nobody wished to admit or even discuss publicly?

Why was Somalia so important for humanitarian reasons when similar conditions affected other nearby African nations?

And, was there a hidden economic agenda that was camouflaged by morality and humanitarianism in order to achieve financial goals?

The answers to these questions as well as many others, lie in the enigma of Somalia, the intrigues of the United Nations, the naivete' of a U.S. administration that failed to recognize the political and military whirlpool into which it was being sucked, and the unwillingness of a semi-aboriginal society to allow its own destiny to be dictated by foreigners.

On March 25, 1994 after the loss of 45 Americans in Somalia during more than a year of operating under dangerous and disease-ridden conditions, the last U.S. force--a rear guard detachment of United States Marines--pushed off the beach in amphibious vehicles and left Somalia.

The remnants of the U.N. force departed a short time later under sniper fire, withdrawing in front of mobs of looters who pounced upon everything left behind.

Doorway to Hell

By the spring of 1994, Somalia had become a disaster. Those most responsible, fearing public exposure and repercussions, used their resources to shift the attention of the public to other matters, such as Rwanda and Bosnia-Herzegovina.

By playing the trump card--Human Suffering--the media, and consequently the minds of the public, could be politically redirected. In words now known by the American people as meaning psychological redirection, the UN, and the U.S. Government, had become very adept at "Wagging the Dog."

Somalia had also become an enigma.

Despite the reluctance of a U.S. President to declare Somalia to be a combat zone, he was forced to issue two posthumous Medals of Honor to American service personnel.

Although the initiation of the operation was humanitarian, no Humanitarian Service Medals were issued to those participating in Operation Restore Hope, despite the issue of such recognition for hurricane relief in Florida. And despite the length of the operation, size of the commitment, and danger to all who served there, the Pentagon went out of its way to avoid issuing any special recognition to those who served in-country, such as the Southwest Asia campaignl, Kuwaiti Liberation and National Defense Service medal granted to Persian Gulf veterans. As a result, the Army and Marine Corps "grunts" who served in Somalia only wear an Armed Forces Expeditionary Medal, with nothing else certifying where they provided such service, almost as if their own country was ashamed of that service--or trying to hide it by lack of recognition.

When our units returned home, there were no parades or celebrations except by the families of the men and women on the posts to which they returned.

Doorway to Hell

Why were Somalian veterans treated with such disdain as compared to those who enjoyed Saudi-supplied salad bars before they overran the Iraqi army two years before?

Is the experience of Somalia the measure of how we treat our servicemen and women based on the popularity or political acceptability of the harm's way in which we send them?

Years from now nobody except 87,000 American servicemen and women, several thousand allied troops, a virtual legion of U.N. officials and bureaucrats, Somalian farmers, camel herders, and villagers who survived -- 45 American families -- will remember this microcosmic chapter of American and U.N. history. Somalia will eventually be overshadowed by current events and those yet to develop. There will also be many in powerful political positions who hope that it will not even be mentioned and will disappear as a conscious subject, for they don't want their constituents reminded of their in- competence. Except for the record contained herein, and hopefully others like it, perhaps it won't be forgotten. Nor hopefully will the lessons learned there be forgotten as well, or the mistakes repeated.

For those who served, those who performed the mission given them by their leaders--and especially those who paid the supreme sacrifice--only they will understand what so many have learned before.

Somalia *is* the Doorway to Hell.

Doorway to Hell

TABLE OF CONTENTS

Doorway to Hell

Chapter One

Sixteen Hours on No Name Street

"Where the hell are they coming from?," yelled an American
Ranger sergeant to a team member as they both hunkered down
in the dirt behind the bullet-pocked wall of the Olympic Hotel in
downtown Mogadishu, Somalia.

"I don't know," his teammate screamed back over the
chattering of automatic weapons fire, "But the bastards are
coming out of the cracks, and I'm getting low on ammo!"

"Yeah, me too! And if we don't get some help pretty quick,
we ain't gettin' out of here!"

In the east African coastal city, it was the hot and humid
afternoon of Sunday, October 3, 1993 and the officers and men
of the U.S. Army's Task Force Ranger, commanded by
Lieutenant Colonel Danny McKnight were in what one of them
described as "deep kimchi."

The scene was right out of a Hollywood war movie.
Automatic weapons fire peppered the walls and smashed the few

4

intact windows still left in the hotel as the Rangers regrouped, helicopters were being shot down by B-40 rockets fired from Rocket Propelled Grenade launchers from adjacent buildings, and grenades were being lobbed into the hotel and adjacent buildings held by the Americans by every Somali within throwing distance. Shortly after Ranger Specialist Fourth Class Carlos Rodriguez rappelled down a rope from a hovering UH-60 Blackhawk helicopter to join a security patrol in a nearby street adjacent to the Olympic Hotel, the Somali guerrillas opened fire. Spotting a Somali gun barrel poke around the corner of a building, he shot at it. Almost immediately, he was hit in the right hip, then lifted into the air by an explosion and slammed into the ground, breaking several bones in the impact.

In the same exchange of gunfire, Rodriguez' squad leader was also hit, forcing the survivors of the patrol to drag the wounded into the temporary safety of a nearby building. As they fought with what they had, guerrillas began to mass around the battle area in clusters, inching closer as the volume of American fire began to slacken. The Americans, not expecting to become engaged in a lengthy firefight when they began the mission, were beginning to run low on ammo. And there was no contingency plan to get them out.

Earlier that same day and not long before breakfast in the U.S. compound, Somali spies on the payroll of the Central Intelligence Agency reported that the subject of the raid, Mohammed Aidid's foreign minister, along with his political advisor and propaganda chief, were holding a meeting in the Olympic Hotel in the Wardigley District of Mogadishu that afternoon. The district was a sprawling neighborhood of walled compounds and alleys that held at least 50,000 people loyal to Aidid. Seemingly, the HUMINT[1] report was verified by the National Security Agency that picked up a radio transmission corroborating the meeting. Mohammed Aidid, the principal warlord among the Somalian clans was a wanted man[2].

What were American Rangers doing in a firefight in Mogadishu, on a street with no name, in a fight for their lives?

Boutros Boutros Ghali, Secretary General of the United Nations and Mohammed Aidid personally disliked one another.. Just a few weeks before, Aidid's gunmen ambushed and killed twenty-eight Pakistani soldiers. This enraged the Secretary General and the UN Security Council. With Ghali's approval, the UN's Deputy Commander in Somalia, retired U.S. Navy Admiral Jonathon Howe, announced that the U.N. would pay a $25,000 reward for information leading to Aidid's arrest. This act did little to endear Aidid and his supporters to accepting UN "peace" and "nation-building" initiatives.

Shortly after the death of the Pakistanis, an American Delta Force unit,[3] attempted to capture Aidid, but he fled Mogadishu and ultimately sought refuge in Nigeria before the mission could be accomplished. In a repetition of what happened in Saigon, Republic of South Vietnam on April 30, 1975, 281 diplomats and U.S. Marine guard personnel had to be airlifted from the besieged U.S. embassy in Mogadishu as armed gangs scaled the walls of the American compound with ladders. The humiliating evacuation operation was not mentioned in the media due to the concentration of media resources on the looming war with Iraq in the Persian Gulf.

The end of the regime had become evident to the nation long before Barre left Mogadishu. The police force, local militia, government ministries, People's Assembly, schools, and hospitals had long since ceased operations. Oil companies evacuated their technicians and crews when warlord gunmen and bandits raided their installations. With the fall of Barre no clear leader appeared on the scene. Finally, on July 15, 1991, six Somali factions agreed to a two-year interim government under the provisions of the old 1961 constitution. With Ali Mahdi Muhammad of the Hawiye clan as President, and Umar Arteh Ghalib of the Isaaq clan as Prime Minister, the new government had to be reorganized because the country had slid into anarchy. No formal infrastructure was left, and the Somalian armed forces had disbanded. Factional fighting between clans prevented the new government from establishing control, and it finally fell as well.

Complicating the problem was the former commander of the Somalian Army, General Mohammad Farah Aidid, who opposed the presidency of Ali Mahdi Muhammad and eventually organized an armed faction of the USC. Compounding that challenge was the opposition of the SSDF and SPM who, believing they were disenfranchised by the provisional government, aligned themselves against the USC.

Fighting erupted between the various factions and clans, and control of Kismayu and Baidoa became objectives in the early stages. The populations of both urban areas suffered greatly from the fighting and the deprivation they endured as a result of the interdiction of their markets and distribution system. The southern and central clan leaders realized the country was beginning to sink into an economic and political abyss. A number of cease fires were negotiated and announced between early 1991 and the latter part of 1992.

However, in the north the SNM refused to participate in the negotiations proposed by the USC, and in May, 1991, it proclaimed the creation of the Republic of Somaliland as an interim government in what had principally been British Somaliland. Decreeing the Islamic Sharia to be the basis of the Republic's law, the SNM unsuccessfully attempted to establish its authority throughout the region. Furthermore, the provisional government was unable to acquire recognition from any foreign nation, thus adding to the chaos that was enveloping the country.

By September 1991, Somalia had become a country with no semblance of government, civil society, or essential services. Food supplies dwindled, vegetables and fruit were infested with worms and insects, water sources were poisoned and contaminated, the telephone system was defunct, the army and police force had disbanded, and hospitals and schools shut down. Somalian society rapidly disintegrated into anarchy and clan violence increased. Somalian currency inflated to the point of being valueless and serious fighting intensified by November.

With the end of March, 1992, more than 14,000 Somalis had been killed and 27,000 wounded in what had become a clan-based civil war. Those who were not killed or wounded suffered from the results of a two-year long drought that devastated Somalian agriculture. Meanwhile, diplomatic efforts by the French colony of Djibouti, the League of Arab States, the Organization of African Unity, the Organization of the Islamic Conference, and the United Nations were unsuccessful in attempting to negotiate an end to the fighting. By early 1993 it was estimated that more than 4.5 million Somalis needed assistance to survive, and about half of those were critical.

By mid-October 1993, 350,000 to 500,000 Somalis had died, and 700,000 were displaced and completely dependent upon outside assistance. Additionally, there were 540,000 Somali refugees in bordering countries who also required assistance. Most of the more critical in Somalia were located in the Gedo and lower-Jubba river regions. U.S. and civilian relief officials estimated that one-fourth of Somalia's children under the age of five had already died and an entire generation of children was in jeopardy. Over 40 percent of the city of Baidoa was already dead, with the rest dying at the rate of several hundred per day.

Despite the presence of relief agencies such as the American Red Cross, Red Crescent Society, CARE International, Doctors Without Borders, Save The Children, SwedeRelief, Irish Concern, and numerous others, warlord bandits, gunmen, and lawlessness disrupted humanitarian efforts. Supply convoys continued to be ambushed. Stockpiles were plundered at gunpoint, and relief agency officials were murdered. By the end of October 1993, all American relief workers departed from Mogadishu, although many others remained on duty throughout the countryside in spite of the threat. By then, CBS's Dan Rather had reported from Mogadishu and declared Somalia to be "Absolutely the worst place on earth."

It was into this cauldron that UN bureaucrats decided to send military forces--bureaucrats who failed to remember the ancient Indian proverb: "Beware, he who rides the tiger, for he may end up *inside* the beast."

Chapter Two

Operation Restore Hope - 1992

Somalian politics are family matters. To understand the spider web of tribal/family government factions, one must understand the clans and the war lords of this Islamic feudal system that are involved in the upper caste power plays.

Ali Mahdi Mohammed (member of the Abgaal clan of the Hawiye clan family and leader of one USC faction) commanded five thousand clansmen and held control of northern Mogadishu as long as his "army" was powerful enough to maintain its presence. He was, however, eventually challenged by a former Somalian army commander named General Mohammed Farah Aidid, of the Habar Gidir clan of the Hayiye clan family. He led the main body of the USC into Mogadishu from their basecamps in Somalia. Aidid's force of ten thousand guerrillas took control of the southern half of the city and advocated cooperation with the SNM. The two factions fought incessantly and turned Mogadishu into a Somalian form of Beirut.

Simultaneously, Siad Barre's brother-in-law Mohammed Siad Hirsi known as "General Morgan," established a force in the southern port city of Kismayu. A former key Somalian army commander, he had been accused of conducting genocide against a minority clan prior to the fall of Siad Barre. He was opposed by Colonel Omar Jess, a renegade army colonel who was in control of Kismayu when U.S. forces moved into the strategic port. Jess was allied with General Aidid's forces in Mogadishu. Just prior to the arrival of U.S. Marines, Jess had hundreds of Morgan's supporters massacred.

Responding to the massacre, in the latter part of February 1993, Morgan secretly led his forces into the city, recovered buried weapons, and attacked Jess's forces. In two weeks of bitter fighting, he pushed Colonel Jess and his forces out of their Kismayu strongholds. The fighting led to anti-American riots in Mogadishu where many Somalis believed that the Americans were supporting a return of Siad Barre. U.S. Marines finally separated both warlords in Kismayu and established an uneasy truce. Morgan and Jess were placed under surveillance, but members of both clans remained within the city limits near the weapons they buried for future use.

No attempt would be made to search for those weapons. Seizing weapons could increase the danger for U.S. troops, which was acknowledged by Robert Oakley, former ambassador to Somalia and a former member of the U.S. delegation to South Vietnam. He said, "There's bound to be a certain amount of hostility since we're disarming people, and at the moment, those being disarmed have no other source of livelihood. The way in which a lot of these so-called armies or gangs make their living was sort of medieval-style by going out and looting. You go out and go to war and you grab the booty from the people you defeat." This was an odd position for Oakley to announce since elsewhere, weapons caches were being captured.

11

Doorway to Hell

Food distribution was also a source of power among the clans as a weapon to control the population. Gunmen, often under the influence of khat, a narcotic weed that was chewed to achieve a "high" and recognizing no authority except that of their own clan leader or warlord, ravaged the countryside. Not only shipments of food to the interior were raided, but also warehouses in Mogadishu were stripped at gunpoint. On November 24, 1992, a relief ship carrying ten thousand tons of food was driven back to sea after being shelled in Mogadishu harbor. The rise of local warlords who controlled the urban areas and cities, as opposed to clan leaders and elders who were more dedicated to peace and negotiation, became a new phenomenon in Somalian society.

Vast quantities of arms and ammunition, previously supplied by the Soviets and the U.S. to the former Somalian armed forces, were readily available. Virtually every Somali male had received formal training on the use of such weaponry, as the Siad Barre regime had required all civil servants plus public school and university students to undergo military training prior to the fall of the regime. The result was that the Somali citizenry was well armed and trained to handle military equipment, a situation that would result in prolonged clan fighting.

In response to the increasingly critical situation, United Nations Secretary General Boutros-Ghali had previously announced in August, 1992 that he would send UN forces into Somalia to protect food supplies. Since, in his previous capacity as an Egyptian diplomat, he had been a friend of Siad Barre, the Somalian clans despised him and the United Nations which he represented. Somali spokesmen representing various warlords objected and warned Boutros-Ghali that the UN force would be resisted. To reinforce the UN Secretary General, President Bush ordered a food airlift to Somalia.

Doorway.to Hell

On August 28 Boutros-Ghali authorized sending 3,500 personnel in addition to a 500-man Pakistani force previously approved for deployment to Somalia. The UN mandate was insufficient to establish a secure environment due not only to the Somali clans' armed opposition to what they perceived as Boutros-Ghali's interference in their internal affairs, but also to the weak and inadequate size of the UN force and the restrictive rules of engagement. Finally, following a series of delays created by warlords in Mogadishu, Pakistani troops were allowed to enter the airport on November 10th.

Eleven days later the United States National Security Council recommended to U.S. President George Bush that U.S. forces should be deployed to Somalia to reinforce the UN effort. Their recommendation was based on the fact that the scale of human disaster was such that the only hope for the Somali people lay in ending the clan fighting and restoring order. The National Security Council advised President Bush that the United States was the only nation perceived by the Somalis and by the region as possessing the ability to launch the necessary large scale aid operation. Based on this apparent rationale and reinforced by daily television coverage of starving Somali children with extended bellies, President Bush authorized the commitment of American forces and called the effort "Operation Restore Hope." He then used his influence to encourage the military commitment of twenty other nations to participate as well.

On December 4, 1992, President Bush ordered twenty-eight thousand American troops to Somalia, East Africa, in support of the United Nations' launching of the world's largest humanitarian rescue. It would be an attempt to feed thousands of starving Somalian people and subdue gunmen who were raiding relief agencies.

13

Although the U.S. provided the bulk of troops, other nations also participated. France committed two-thousand troops from the 13th French Foreign Legion from Djibouti and the 9th Regiment of French Marines, Italy promised troops and aid, and the African nations of Nigeria, Kenya, and Zimbabwe also announced that they would send troops. In making the commitment, President Bush assured the American people that U.S. forces would "be home by Inauguration Day."

The administration should have known better. U.S. military advisors had been previously assigned to Somalia as late as 1985 and the veterans of that commitment knew the character and challenges of the country. Anyone who had served in Somalia then could have told anyone who would listen that the time chosen couldn't have been worse in terms of the weather. December is midsummer in Somalia and temperatures at the equator, which cuts across the country at Kismayu south of Mogadishu, exceed a hundred degrees in the daytime with humidity surpassing seventy percent. Furthermore, a drought had affected the region for several years, and Somalia had received insufficient rain to support its small amount of arable land.

Meanwhile, orders were sent from the Pentagon to Headquarters of Central Command (CENTCOM) located in Tampa, Florida. Under the command of General Joseph Hoar, who replaced General H. Norman Schwarzkopf following the Persian Gulf War, CENTCOM sent deployment alert orders to subordinate units designated as critical to the mission. Hoar also made one other decision. Unlike Schwarzkopf, he decided not to move CENTCOM's headquarters to Somalia. Instead, he designated his Deputy Commander, Major General Thomas Montgomery, as commanding general of all U.S. military forces in Somalia and Deputy Commander of UN forces. Montgomery's headquarters would represent CENTCOM

The displacement became CENTCOM's Headquarters-Forward in Somalia and maintain communications with Hoar in

14

Tampa via satellite. Dividing headquarters between rear echelon senior commanders and lower echelon on-scene commanders was a decision that had proven catastrophic in the past, and would again in Somalia.

The trucks and Humvees of the 4th Marine Service Support Group began rolling down the palm tree-lined roads of Camp Pendleton, California soon after word of the deployment was received on December 4th. Air contingency forces are routinely maintained at Pendleton on a sixteen-hour alert status, and the initial mission summary made it clear that this operation's logistical needs determined the sequence in which the units were sent. During the past summer, the Camp Pendleton Marines had conducted an exercise involving off-loading ships. Now that training would pay off.

At Fort Drum, New York, just south of the Canadian border, the U.S. Army's 10th Mountain Division received the same deployment order. The Division, subject to an eighteen-hour alert status as part of the Army's rapid-reaction 18th Airborne Corps, immediately put its Ready Force One on notice. One of five highly mobile light divisions in the Army, the 10th can deploy its assets by air. However, it was also charged with replacing an Army headquarters as the chief logistical support within the Somalian theater. Consequently it would need supplies and equipment sent to Somalia aboard fast transport ships.

When the 10th Division's Ready Force One rumbled out of the gates of Fort Drum on December 9th, it was, like the Marines, front-loaded with logistics, support units, and mobility assets. Unlike the Marines in California, however, the soldiers of the 10th departed their base in northern New York during a heavy blizzard.

Doorway to Hell

At Fort Benning, Georgia, the designated units of the Army's 36th Engineer Group began packing and loading their equipment. Personnel processing centers were established where wills were updated, powers of attorney were signed, physical and dental exams were conducted, inoculations were administered, and life insurance and next-of-kin designations were updated. A year before, they went to Desert Storm followed by duty in Florida after Hurricane Andrew, so many of the troops were familiar with the drill.

While the military began to carry out its mission, the overall operation was not without political opposition. Congressman John Murtha (D-PA), Chairman of the U.S. House Defense Appropriations Subcommittee said, "The United States should not put large numbers of troops into Somalia, because America can only afford so much, and no one can predict how long they would stay. I don't think we have the resources. Military intervention in Somalia is not in America's long-term interest and will place too much pressure on the strapped defense budget."

Despite Murtha's open opposition, President-elect Bill Clinton gave his tacit approval to Bush's commitment of U.S. forces. Clinton said in referring to President's Bush's decision, "I share his determination to ensure the success of this important mission. The United Nations operation was evidence that the international community will not stand idly by while armed bandits force starvation on millions of people who become pawns in a political struggle for power."

These were lofty words for a president that "abhorred" the military, and in the next eight years would send the American forces abroad for what later became known as "international meals-on-wheels missions" in such places as Macedonia, Bosnia and Kosovo. The Clinton-Gore administration would not only overextend our military forces, but reduce our military in strength, equipment, and logistics to the breaking point. The operations in Somalia would demonstrate what would happen when a military force is used for "operations other than war," as the Pentagon began calling "peacetime" U.N. and NATO operations. To paraphrase General Schwarzkopf, the military is designed to go places, break things and kill people. It is not designed to administer civilian and population control functions or manage civil government on a long term basis. Somalia would become a prime example of this.

Clinton was also in an awkward situation. He was well aware of being on public record during the recent bitter presidential campaign as criticizing Bush for failing to take action in Somalia, a tactical maneuver presumably designed to appeal to the African-American voting bloc, an overwhelming majority of whom voted for Clinton. Additionally, the articulated goal to save the Somalian people from starvation as stated by President Bush was morally unassailable.

However, other politicians from both political parties objected as well. Opposition generated from those who had neither substantial African-American voting blocs in their district or states, or who could foresee the potential pit into which the United States might be injecting itself, came from both sides of the aisle   .

On the same day that President-elect Clinton issued his support statement, Murtha again blasted the commitment, "You're talking $400 million a month, maybe a billion dollars. We've got homeless people in this country. The last election was all about the economy. This is a fundamental change in policy. We've always sent troops because of a national threat. Where does it stop--Russia or, Sarajevo?."

Doorway to Hell

Joining Murtha from the other side of the Congressional aisle, during a speech in Topeka, Kansas, United States Senator Robert Dole (R-KS), Senate Minority Leader, said, "The United States cannot afford to start a 911-USA service to deliver humanitarian aid around the world. I think the thing that bothers me most is where do we go next? If somebody knocks on the door next week and says that they have people starving, does that become the new mission for our armed forces, to go around the world, and sort of be the policeman for everybody and making certain that everybody is properly fed?."

Despite the reservations expressed by Murtha, Dole, and others in influential positions in both parties, the U.S. military went to work carrying out the President's orders. Within twenty-four hours, three U.S. Navy ships carrying a brigade of Marines left the island of Diego Garcia[4] in the Indian Ocean and set sail for the Somalian coast.

On December 8, 1992. U.S. reconnaisance jets flew over Mogadishu and photographed the city and possible landing areas in the vicinity. Meanwhile Robert Oakley, a special U.S. envoy and former U.S. Ambassador to Somalia, was restating the mission as being one of "humanitarian all the way through, because the purpose is to protect deliveries of relief supplies, relief recipients, and relief workers." However, it was already obvious that Boutros-Ghali had a different agenda in mind.

Two days before Oakley articulated what American troops would be doing, Boutros Ghali appeared before the Conference on Global Development at the Carter Center and stated: "After distribution of food, the gangs will disappear. The U.N. will then broker aggressive peace negotiations with the warring Somali clans. We will need massive assistance in reconstruction, in creating a police force, and in resettling refugees." This statement should have alerted those who were in the audience to the fact that Boutros Boutros-Ghali had a longer-range mission in mind than merely saving Somalians from starvation. Reconstruction of a country required the establishment of a government and that could only be done with the approval and support of the Somalis. As events would prove, the Somalis were not about to bow to a government imposed upon them by the UN or anyone else. And what later became extremely ironic about Ghali's stance on Somalia as a peacemaker, is the fact that while working for the Egyptian government as foreign minister, he was the principle bureaucrat that sold $5.8 millions of dollars of military weapons to the pagan Hutu tribe of Rwanda. That sale led to the genocidal massacre of millions of Christian Tutsi tribesmen. This proved the United Nations, who eventually sent African troops but did not intervene in the killings, was an impotent force without US aid, troops and leadership.

As the UN troops steamed toward East Africa, Somalian gangs engaged in a last-minute rampage and stole half of the stored food already in Somalia and waiting for distribution. Fighting erupted in Kismayu, Mogadishu, Bardera, and Baidoa in what the clan leaders perceived as their last chance to gain control of areas not yet secured by their enemies. With the prospect of the arrival of the troops, the gun market in Mogadishu collapsed. AK-47 automatic rifles that had been imported from the USSR and China dropped in price overnight from $400 to $30 per weapon.

Shortly after midnight, Wednesday, December 9th, U.S. Navy SEALS and Marines landed to the unwelcome glare of television strobe lights illuminating them and their landing site. One Marine snarled at a cameraman as he hustled by, "I almost shot you, you stupid son of a bitch! I thought it was muzzle flashes!

Doorway to Hell

The Marines overran the beach at Half Moon Bay and entered Mogadishu. The world watched the landing via satellite television coverage provided by international news teams who were waiting for the invasion force.

As the small reconnaissance units slipped into the sleeping Somali capital under the light of a full moon, they entered a cove adjacent to Mogadishu International Airport. The troops hauled in two inflatable rafts filled with their equipment-laden packs. They scurried across the beach toward bunkers as photographers and cameramen chased them with lights and cameras through the dunes and brush. Carrying portable illumination, the reporters attempted to interview the stone-faced, grease-painted men to the rage of family members in the United States who perceived the media as compromising the security of their loved ones.

Prior to the landings, General Aidid and Mohammed Madi used Somalian radio to broadcast a warning to their troops to avoid the Mogadishu airport and port facility. UN officials instructed two-hundred foreign relief workers to stay indoors for at least twenty-four to forty-eight hours. With the arrival of U.S. troops, the Somali shilling, long a ridiculous currency pegged by an armed cartel at seven thousand to the dollar, increased in value overnight to four thousand to the dollar due to trading on the Mogadishu markets.

While the Marines were securing the capital, an order arrived at Fort Benning, Georgia, alerting Colonel Philip Anderson, Commander of the U.S. Army's 36th Engineer Group that elements of his force were to prepare for deployment to Somalia. Subsequent orders were passed down the chain of command. One of the recipients was Lieutenant Colonel Robert L. "Larry" Davis, Commander-43rd Engineer Combat Battalion (Heavy).

Doorway to Hell

The assignment would not be new to Davis or the engineers of the 43rd. They had been through humanitarian operations before. Many of them had participated in the relief and clean-up efforts in Florida after the devastating results of Hurricane Andrew became apparent and state resources were overwhelmed. Some members of the 43rd had also been involved in road-building and other assignments in Honduras, so one more humanitarian mission before the Battalion was due to inactivate in the summer of 1994 was just routine for the Engineers of the 43d. Other units in the 36th Engineer Group,the parent unit of the 43d at Fort Benning, also received an alert order from Anderson were the Group Headquarters and Headquarters Company, 63rd Engineer Company, elements of the 535th Engineer Detachment, the 608th Ordnance Company, and the 498th and 690th Medical Companies.

The Christmas holidays soon took on a different meaning as the men and women assigned to those commands began packing MILVANS--huge box containers that fit on the bed of a flat-bed semi-truck--and preparing their personal equipment for what many believed to be certain deployment. Those requiring shots received them, and because of the disease factor in Somalia, additional shots beyond normal overseas deployment standards were required. Most of the troops stood the basic battery of shots, but with the extra shots they received for Somalia, some of them fainted on the spot and others were sick for several days. Captain Jeff King, assistant plans officer for the 36th Group Headquarters was typical. He said, "I was maxed out and received five shots." Included among them was gamma globulin which is the 'ultimate' inoculation for the most disease-ridden regions of the world.

While the 36th Engineers were receiving their inoculations, MTT's (Mobile Training Teams) from the Engineer School at

21

Doorway to Hell

Fort Leonard Wood, Missouri, went to Fort Benning to provide training on newly-issued mine detectors, mine identification, and MCAP (Mine Clearing Armor Protection) system (an armor-plated kit that covers and offers mine protection capability to the D-7 bulldozer).

Although the 43rd had been alerted and was told it was going to Somalia, no mission had been sent with the alert order. This was in spite of the personal appearance at Fort Benning of Chairman of the Joint Chiefs of Staff General Colin Powell who delivered remarks about the nature of the overall mission.

With no guidance as to what they were supposed to do when they arrived, LTC Davis could only guess what would be required of his troops upon arrival. So, to cover the possibilities, he ordered the Battalion's construction section to design generic base camps for 500, 1,000, 2,500, and 5,000 soldiers and prepare a bill of materials. Realizing that there was no supply of construction materials in Somalia, FORSCOM gave approval to acquire the supplies that would be needed to build two 1,000 soldier basecamps. The contract for plywood, culverts, cement, and dimensioned lumber amounted to $1.7 million. The materials were loaded into 129 twenty and forty-foot Milvans which were then hauled to Savannah by contract truckers.

While Anderson's 36th Engineers were preparing for deployment, the operation in Somalia was well underway. Meanwhile, U.S. Marines, supported by Pakistani troops, had secured the airport. Mogadishu was quiet and food shipments had already begun arriving. Virtually overnight the arrival of U.S. troops raised expectations among the Somalis that an end to their terror and starvation was in sight.

Everywhere they turned, American Marines and soldiers found themselves hemmed in by Somalis eager to touch

American flesh, gesture their relief, and smile their thanks. Declared thirty-two-year-old Fatima Mohammed, the mother of seven, "I'd like the U.S. troops to stay here for life."

Though the Americans were initially feared, many of the Somalis soon overcame that reaction and began to look upon them as liberators. In Afgoi, Hawa Abdi, a doctor with the International Committee of the Red Cross said, "Before American troops arrived, we had the idea that the military would bring only destruction and killing, but the American troops bring food, they play with the children, we have more security, and we don't wish that they will leave."

That was precisely the problem. The Somalis expected nothing short of an African Marshall Plan. They wanted the Americans to stay long enough to fix not only their diet, but their broken government and lawless society.

In the headlong rush to save the Somali people though, no thought was given to providing for Somali animals. Without feed and medicine for the animals, Somali farmers faced a potential catastrophe even where they might be able to obtain seed to raise grain. Sleeping sickness and rinderpest were already epidemic among the remaining cattle that had been kept safe from rustlers during the civil war. Veterinary services had collapsed throughout the country, and without available chemicals to spray for the deadly tsetse fly the Somali cattle were doomed. "They just forgot the animals," said Omar Ali Alinashe, a British-trained veterinarian whose drug stocks were down to human pain pills. He added, "Somalia is finished without its livestock. You can feed people now, but if you don't save their livestock and crops, what do they eat next? Two thirds of Somali exports are livestock. Without that, there is no income."

Doorway to Hell

Political considerations simply were not focused on animals or how the Somali people would support themselves. The primary concern was food distribution and security. Even that objective was generic in terms of its articulation. The UN resolution authorizing the use of military forces was purposely vague on disarming the clan gunmen who were the primary threat to food distribution and security. Equally vague were the directives given the military commanders on the ground regarding the disarming of the gunmen. When pressed to articulate what guidelines existed, Robert Oakley, a native Virginian and former State Department official in Vietnam who had been appointed U.S. special envoy to Somalia replied, "We plan to negotiate with the Somalis and have them do it." Few of the troops that were already on the ground in Somalia considered that a practical policy. They had already discovered in the brief time they had been there that Somalia was in chaos and anybody who had the most force was in charge.

That lack of direction left the military forces in an open-ended situation where parameters on proper action sometimes had to be decided in micro-seconds, depending upon the threat. Within two days of the arrival of the U.S. Marines and French Foreign Legionnaire paratroopers in Mogadishu, two Somalis were killed at a French checkpoint when a loaded truck attempted to run their roadblock. At the same time, a large convoy of "technicals"[5], small pickup trucks carrying clan guerrillas equipped with heavy pedestal mounted machine guns, automatic weapons and grenades, was spotted heading west from the Baidoa area toward the Ogaden region of eastern Ethiopia where they would be provided refuge by Somalis living there.

On December 13th, U.S. Marines made a food run into northern Mogadishu and in the process engaged three armed "technicals" in a firefight. Combat helicopters poured a withering fire on the "technicals" and destroyed them, leaving their occupants dead or wounded. The U.S. convoy continued to its destination with the twenty-two tons of food it carried. Consequently, the convoy served as much as an object lesson as it was a delivery. It demonstrated to the gunmen that the Marines could go anywhere they wished in Mogadishu if unfettered by political or upper echelon intervention or "rules of engagement" which were later changed on almost a daily basis.

One person who was not awed was General Mohammed Farah Aidid. He took careful notes about how the UN forces responded to each provocation and laid plans for what tactics he would use in the future.

Chapter Three

Conflict of Purpose

It was not long before bitter debate had began about the military's role in Somalia. Secretary of State Lawrence Eagleburger, still serving in the lame duck Bush administration, was forced to deny publicly that there was a disagreement with the United Nations over the scope of U.S. efforts. He acknowledged, however, that Boutros Ghali had sent President Bush a private letter setting out aims for the mission.

They included the disarming of the Somali clan gunmen, a mission not specified in the UN resolution authorizing the use of military force in Somalia--and definitely one the Somalis would resist. It was already obvious that Boutros Ghali had a different agenda in mind than did President Bush, and the Secretary General knew that he wouldn't have to deal with Bush after Inauguration Day when William Jefferson Clinton of Arkansas would succeed as President. Unknowingly, the American people and military had been set up by the UN--and the ramifications could be devastating.

Doorway to Hell

In response to the debate that was going on at the highest echelons between the UN leadership and U.S. political and military leaders, Major General Robert Johnston, the American Marine commander in Somalia, felt obligated to state that his goal was not to disarm Somalia. On NBC's news program "Meet The Press," he said, "I have a rather precisely described mission, to establish the right security environment to allow for the free movement of relief supplies. If I am given a new mission, then I will pursue that mission. At this point, I have had no change in orders."

In reality, "establishing the right security environment" gave Johnston a wide latitude to interpret that phrase in whatever manner he chose. As events later proved, he construed it to expand the involvement of the U.S. in Somalian affairs. This interpretation lent itself conveniently to Boutros Ghali's agenda.

At the United Nations, Boutros Ghali vigorously replied to the press: "Disarming the Somali factions is very important, to provide the security which will allow us to replace the unified command with a UN peacekeeping operation."

U.S. officials, however, did not want their forces bogged down in pacifying a country which was bristling with trigger-happy gunmen and weapons caches. The debate behind closed doors continued while the troops tried to provide some semblance of order in the middle of a Somalian national disaster. While negotiations continued, the situation in Somalia had changed from one of "hands across the sea" to one of an increasing resentment by the warlords that would prove disastrous to American forces. For by this time American troops were beginning to find out that many of the locals were not so appreciative and friendly. Instead our troops became subjected to harassing small arms and mortar fire, ambushes, land mines, booby traps and sniper fire. This was not what they had

27

expected when they were sent on a "humanitarian relief mission." And it would get worse.

The U.S. Military was beginning to feel like they were caught in the middle of a mission that was about to change. And they weren't happy. Did Boutros Ghali put America on the path of "riding the tiger?" The last tiger America rode without total support of the American people was Vietnam, and because of that, as soon as bodybags began to pile up, such an adventure would be doomed to failure at the outset.

The American military, if they had not forgotten the lessons of the Vietnam War, would realize that to be successful in a Third World military operation, they would have to win the "hearts and minds" of not only the Somalis, but the American people as well. And landing troops to physically disarm tribesmen with warrior mentalities and no fear of death had the potential be become a deadly quagmire at best, and a bloody debacle at worst. U.S. commanders did not want to find themselves in a position where the UN was willing to fight to the last American.

On December 16th, U.S. Marines and French Foreign Legionnaires entered the devastated desert city of Baidoa. Prior to their arrival, the Red Crescent Society[6] (the Moslem version of the Red Cross) was forced to take time from their relief efforts to bury two hundred bodies per day. When there was finally enough food, the immune systems of the Baidoans and the refugees flooding the city had already eroded to such a degree that they were susceptible to diseases. Dysentery, diarrhea, hepatitis, bronchitis, and measles that could be easily treated in a western country proved deadly to thousands in Baidoa.

Doorway to Hell

When food began to reach Baidoa, the city of forty thousand became a magnet for refugees, and virtually overnight the population increased to eighty-thousand, with thousands more overloading the capacities of surrounding villages. The refugees brought disease with them. Soon, epidemics began to kill more people than were dying of starvation, and starvation itself was still taking a terrible toll.

The average Somali adult's caloric intake had dropped from 1,200 calories per day in 1988 to a hopelessly inadequate 200 per day. Many suffered from blindness due to a lack of Vitamin A, and young girls were doomed to be childless because of malformed pelvises. Michael D'Armo of Catholic Relief Services observed, "Even when they are fed and back on their feet, there'll be an entire generation of kids suffering from mental retardation."

Baidoa in Somalian means "place of bones." It was well-named. The city was a center of utter horror.

Unburied bodies were in the streets, bloated from the heat and used as a breeding source by flies and other insects. The Marines and Legionnaires who had been in combat zones before recognized the sickening aroma of death long before they sighted the city. Besides the bodies in the streets, those that had already been buried in shallow graves of sand were already partially uncovered by the monsoons and wind.. The surviving Somalis didn't have the strength or the equipment to dig deep graves. They laid out the dead and covered them with sand and rocks. As the rains and wind swept over the shallow graves, portions of the decomposing bodies would protrude. Finding rotting flesh, insects would deposit their larvae and breed more insects which would serve as an ongoing regeneration of disease. Baidoa, to the first arriving allied troops, had the appearance of a WW I battlefield with rotting arms, legs and skulls emerging from the ground as "far as I could see" according to one Marine on the advance party. Another Marine in the point element that reached Baidoa and who was a veteran of the Persian Gulf War, vomited from the sight of horror and misery and the smell of death and rotting flesh.

After setting up a security perimeter to protect themselves against Somali gunmen, the second mission of the first troops to arrive in what was described by an English-speaking French Foreign Legionnaire as "a black hole of Hell," was to dig a mass grave and re-bury an estimated *30,000 bodies*.

Insect life was a real threat in what the Royal Australian Infantry Regiment referred to as the "Outback." Swarms of insects would attack soldiers while they were asleep, attracted by the carbon dioxide exhaled from their lungs or the odor of their perspiration. Double layers of mosquito netting would help but would not prevent attack when the soldier arose and had to emerge from his netted cocoon. Some soldiers and Marines had no netting and were subject to constant assaults by insects that are among the most aggressive in the world.

A typical example was that of the tumbu fly. The Somalian tumbu fly is born in a cradle of sand and human excrement.
The fly then searches for a host body, often human, then burrows under the host's skin where its eggs develop into maggots. When a maggot grows large enough, it chews its way through the skin, crawls out and finds a patch of mud to complete its metamorphisis into a tumbu fly.

One morning an American army sergeant awoke to find a lump under his skin. He thought it was just a bug bite. It was, but he didn't realize that he'd been bitten by the tumbu fly. He ignored it until the pain became too much to bear.

Doorway to Hell

Navy Commander Mehdi Pakzad, a doctor at the joint task force aid station, first thought the lump under the sergeant's skin was an infected insect bite. After antibiotics failed, he reexamined the lump. "When I touched it, it jumped back," he said. The doctor surgically removed the lump after he realized it was a tumbu fly larvae.

At least two Americans were "implanted" by Somalian tumbu flies, and two Somali workers were treated for wounds when the insects ate their way out of the workers' bodies. Rubber bands became popular as a form of amusement because soldiers could use them to "pick off" flies when they settled on any surface. In one Marine company, a Marine asked his family back home to send him an air pistol. During down times, he and his buddies would practice their marksmanship skills by shooting BBs at the insects that accumulated inside their tents.

Somalia was unique in that it possessed insect and animal life straight out of a horror movie. Besides the tumbu fly, U.S. and allied troops had to deal with black mamba and cobra snakes, two-inch long red fire ants, six-inch long cockroaches, nine-inch long poisonous centipedes and eighteen-inch long toxic spiders. No wonder that troops in the outback hung their boots on tentpoles at night when they hit the sack.

LTC Stewart Besser, medical officer for the 10th Mountain Division Task Force pronounced Somalia to be "the worst medical environment the U.S. Army had ever served." Malaria struck one Marine and one 10th Mountain soldier shortly after they arrived in-country, and Besser had to inspect washing areas to make sure that stagnant water did not provide breeding grounds for mosquitoes, as well as latrines for flies which would infest such areas within hours. Besser pointed out, "This was the dry season. I'm waiting to see what will happen when the monsoons arrive."

Doorway to Hell

He warned his men to stay away from the termite mounds sprinkled around the landscape, most of which were taller than his soldiers. Somalian termites are as long as a man's forefinger. He warned all personnel, "Don't mess with them or you'll have bugs all over God's creation."

Aggressive poisonous snakes and scorpions the size of a hand invaded the tents and washing areas. Huge centipedes as long as a forearm would also appear from nowhere. Staff Sergeant Stuart James said, "You've got to stab them with a bayonet to kill them, and I'm not kidding."

First Sergeant Daniel Mace of Headquarters and Headquarters Company told his soldiers at a morning formation, "There are so many unknown and exotic diseases in this country, I'm giving you an order: don't touch any animals. Just walk away."

While the troops in the outback battled disease, starvation, the overload of emaciated refugees, insects, snipers, ambushes, land mines, and disease, it was sometimes difficult to remember that this was a humanitarian mission and that the country was also in the middle of a civil war. In Mogadishu, the city rapidly divided between the forces of General Mohammed Aidid in the south and interim President Ali Mahdi Mohammed occupying the north. A zone of demarcation between the two was referred to as the "Green Line," with the main feeding center located in one of Mogadishu's hardest hit areas. Virtually every building in Mogadishu, including Islamic mosques reflected the pock-marked signs of gunfire.

As C5A and C-141 aircraft continued to land at Mogadishu Airport bringing in more troops, supplies, food, and equipment, the gunmen became aware that their power was beginning to slip away. As U.S. forces moved into positions around

Doorway to Hell

Mogadishu and into the outback to the outlying towns of Bale Dogle, Baidoa, Jiliib, Kismayu, Wajiid, Bardera, and Oddur,[7] the guerrillas became more bold. Marines in Mogadishu were subject to increasing sniper attacks and convoys were ambushed at an alarming rate.

Near Afgoi, gunmen armed with AK-47 submachine guns opened fire on a food convoy about thirty-five miles west of Mogadishu. The twelve-vehicle convoy was returning from Baidoa, 120 miles west northwest of Mogadishu. American Marines immediately returned the fire and wounded three Somali gunmen. The ambush took place just as Robert Oakley was being interviewed on "Voice of America" stating that he had warned all clan leaders that "any gunmen found in Mogadishu would be shot." So much for respecting local customs.

However, gunmen weren't the only threat to the Somali people. In the refugee camps in Kenya, despite Islamic religious prohibitions against such assaults, "hundreds" of Somali women were raped by Somali men and Kenyan soldiers guarding the camps. The high incidence of rape is reflective of the second-class status women occupy in Somalian society. Once raped, Somalian women are then ostracized by their own family and exiled. At puberty, about 90 percent of Somali females undergo genital mutilation called infibulation, in which the clitoris and labia minora are removed and the genitals are sewn almost shut to ensure virginity. The procedure is done by older women using razor blades under unsanitary conditions and often results in infection and lifelong pain. A Somali man may have as many as four wives and may immediately divorce a wife if he believes she was not a virgin when she married.

The devastation and horror of the country had a psychological effect on many American troops, a condition which was personally monitored by Dr. David Marlowe, Chief of Military Psychiatry at Walter Reed Army Institute of Research in Washington D.C. Marine Staff Sergeant John Kitchen was a typical example. The first time he saw the "emaciated walking dead, others too weak to move, the smell of death, and the millions of flies, many of them covering the eyes and faces of children," he returned to his quarters and "stared at the wall" for several hours not believing what he had seen. The thirty-six year-old Marine said, "It will remain in my head forever." The U.S. Army dispatched a psychological assessment team before the end of the year to determine what volume and degree of psychological trauma the services would have to deal with and to help the military prepare for such future missions.

The study may help the Army provide the guidance and training to its troops that is necessary to cope with such challenges in the future, but the horror experienced by U.S. troops at the time would bury itself in each soldier's conscience. For months after the U.S. troops returned home, the images of the walking dead and dying remained with them.[8]

During the months following the return of the Somalian veterans, family members and friends reported incidents of flashbacks to the more horrible aspects of the Somalian operation. Also evident were personality changes, irritability, and a tendency to argue irrationally. The soldiers themselves failed to recognize that they were recovering from a psychological shock to their mental and emotional systems. Only time would heal their wounds. (In the case of the 43rd Engineers, just as they were beginning to attain a state of normalcy, they were ordered back to Somalia. This compounded the effect not only on them but also on the families they left behind. Upon their second return they had to begin the recovery process all over again.)

Doorway to Hell

True to his campaign promises and rhetoric, President-elect Bill Clinton attempted to keep his focus on domestic issues as he announced his first appointments to the administration that would take office on January 20th. Yet, as much as the former Arkansas Governor would have wished it otherwise, the world was already beginning to close in on him. Like most newcomers to the oval office, even before he was sworn in, Clinton learned that international events and the actions of his predecessor were setting his agenda. Furthermore, the commitment of American troops to a mission with no apparent national interest at stake instantly opened a debate as to where the new president would take the country, considering his campaign criticism of Bush for not intervening in Somalia prior to the landings.

Clinton's advocacy of U.S. military intervention in Somalia during the campaign came back to haunt him. He had no way of knowing that was exactly what Bush would do after the election by leaving the new President with a major foreign policy headache based on the military commitment to Somalia that Clinton had not only advocated in the campaign but approved. As he took office, he began for the first time to realize that he had to have specific answers to pointed questions as well as a fully-developed foreign policy. At a press conference before Christmas, Clinton displayed an increasing awareness that he was going to be dragged into foreign affairs. He said, "Our administration will be forced to spend a lot of time on foreign policy whether we want to or not." Unfortunately, as events would prove, Clinton had little interest or capability in foreign affairs and didn't spend the time on it he indicated would be necessary. To compound this, he appointed Madeline Albright as his Secretary of State, which would haunt U.S. policy making in the future as she–a female–attempted to negotiate with Moslems, who considered females inferior to men in general, and particularly in government matters. Despite her diplomatic experience, sending her into the Middle East to serve as "point-person" for the White House was insulting to almost every Middle East and Eastern Asia country dominated by Muslims.

Meanwhile, President Bush undertook his twenty-fifth and final foreign overseas trip. This time it was to the Black Sea Conference with Russia's Boris Yeltsin. On the way, Bush visited Mogadishu, becoming the first President since Lincoln to observe hostile fire. On New Year's night, while Bush remained aboard the U.S.S. *Tripoli* (a Navy amphibious assault ship in Mogadishu harbor), the two warlords of Mogadishu lit up the sky with mortar fire and tracer ammunition three miles west of the U.S. Embassy compound. The battle, apparently over an arms cache, killed seventeen Somalis and wounded twenty-five. It was the largest since U.S. forces arrived on December 9th.

The troops in Somalia were at least provided a form of Presidential consolation. Addressing American forces at a military base which served as a food hub in Mogadishu, Bush said: "U.S. troops will stay in Somalia a relatively short time. Our mission is limited in scope and time. Each day you are here you can be proud of what you did for mankind."

His words were not heard by fifty-one year old Lawrence L. Freeman, an American civilian employee of the U.S. AID mission to Somalia. A week before he became the first American to be killed in Somalia when his jeep hit a mine in Mogadishu.

As the world celebrated the new year and most of the Somalian population was just grateful for the fact that they were still alive, engineer Lieutenant Colonel Larry Davis and his troops at Fort Benning, Georgia worked around the clock until the last piece of equipment was loaded. He had pushed his command to load the railcars so they could have as much off time as possible to celebrate the holidays at home with their families. Just before Christmas the Battalion's equipment was finally packed, loaded, and sent to the port of Savannah by rail for shipment to Somalia aboard the transport ship *Bellatrix*.

For four days Davis had commanded an around-the-clock operation to achieve his objective. It was no small task. "You don't realize how big a combat heavy engineer battalion is until you put the whole thing on a train," said First Lieutenant Pablo Ruiz, platoon leader in Bravo Company.

The shipment involved bulldozers, scrapers, graders, cranes, compactors, and dump trucks. The Battalion also loaded forty-seven Milvans with tents, cots, repair parts, food, personal gear, water, and tools.

On January 8th the advance party of the 36th Engineer Group boarded a plane for Mogadishu. Colonel Philip Anderson, the Group Commander, led the party aboard immediately following a farewell ceremony at Fort Benning's Lawson Army Airfield. During the ceremony, Major General Jerry A. White, commander of the post, remarked to the departing engineers: "I know you are going to go over there and do an outstanding job for your country, and the people of Bosnia [sic]." An army spokesman, who declined to be named, said that White's comment was obviously a "slip of the tongue." It was also obviously reflective that more than Somalia was on the General's mind.

Like the war in Vietnam a generation before, civilian criticism was focused on the military. This time however, it was pointed at the brass instead of at the troops on the ground. With 21,000 military personnel in Somalia, the operation was run by a cumbersome top-heavy headquarters consisting of nine generals and one admiral, a ratio of one flag officer for every 2,100 troops.

Doorway to Hell

The Air Force contingent of six hundred airmen was commanded by Brigadier General Thomas Mikolajcik, yet an Army battalion of equivalent size would be commanded by a lieutenant colonel. Two battalions from the Army's 10th Mountain Division were also in-country. The two lieutenant colonels commanding them had more than enough supervision. Also present was Major General Thomas Arnold, commander of the 10th Mountain Division based at Fort Drum, New York. Accompanying him was his assistant division commander for maneuver, Brigadier General Lawson Magruder, and the division chief of staff who was a full colonel, another colonel who commanded the brigade in which both battalions were assigned, and the division operations officer who was a lieutenant colonel awaiting promotion to colonel. In summary, two flag officers, two colonels, and one lieutenant colonel supervised two lieutenant colonels and their two battalions.

Like senior officer rotations through the combat zone during the ten year Vietnam war, it was career ticket punching time once again for the American military officer corps.

The overall commander of U.S. forces was US Marine general Major General Robert Johnston. His headquarters enjoyed the luxury of four general officers and hit a peak strength of one-thousand personnel on December 21, 1992–giving the Marines a general for every 250 troops, a position normally held by a captain. In fact, one of the government-contracted Evergreen Airline 747's was filled entirely with staff officers and clerks for Johnston's headquarters. After landing and disgorging its human cargo, it headed back to the United States to pick up the infantry of the 3rd Battalion, 9th Marines.

It is a truism of military operations that the larger a headquarters is, the more troops are needed to protect it. Marine

Doorway to Hell

Brigadier General Peter Pace, deputy commander of the Marine force in Somalia, complained about the shortage of combat troops to restore order. Yet, an entire Marine rifle company from the lst Marine Division had to be diverted to provide security for Major General Johnston's headquarters.

While civilian newsmen were focusing on Johnston and his headquarters where they conducted interviews in air conditioned offices and composed news reports from press releases handed out by the Public Affairs Officer, the advance party of the 43rd Engineers from Fort Benning quietly arrived aboard an Evergreen 747 on a hot, sultry Monday, January 11th, at Mogadishu Airport. They, in turn, were followed closely by the main body of the Battalion in another aircraft.

The 43rd Engineers arrived in-country still without a specific mission. Only "vague" guidance had been given prior to their departure with reference to "building airfields, basecamps, and roads." Colonel Anderson and LTC Davis immediately met with Colonel Robert Flowers, Chief Engineer of the Joint Task Force, and worked out mission assignments between Army Engineers and the Navy's 30th SeaBee (Construction Battalion) battalion with regard to specific projects. This process proved very valuable because it conserved resources, prioritized effort, and assigned missions. (The procedure would also serve Davis well when the 43rd later returned to Somalia and he found himself the senior Engineer officer in-country.)

Meanwhile the 36th Engineer Group Headquarters, the parent organization of the 43d, located itself in Mogadishu. Engineer Base (later named Hunter Base) was constructed and the base cluster included the 36th Headquarters from Fort Benning, Georgia;

Headquarters and Headquarters Company (HHC) of the 41st Engineer Battalion, and the 710th Main Support Battalion,

10th Mountain Division from Fort Drum, New York. Flood lights, trip flares, triple strand concertina fence, and guard towers were deployed around the base. The base cluster security force ranged from 10 soldiers during daylight hours to 20 personnel during darkness. Security personnel off-duty comprised the base cluster Quick Reaction Force. Bunkers were built for troops not on security missions or part of the QRF. The rest of the personnel within the base also had to remain alert because Somalis who were contracted to perform basic labor assignments would also steal anything they could get their hands on, something that would cost Somali lives at a later date when other UN troops tortured and executed captured thieves.

Meanwhile everyone in the base cluster knew they were constantly under observation. Somali children would play around the base and Somali men and women would watch activities inside the camp. Everything that went on that could be observed from a distance was reported to General Mohammed Farah Aidid, especially when convoys left the enclosure. When Somalis who were contracted to work in the base emerged, they would also report on activities inside the perimeter. As one African-American soldier suggested, "It was as if a white man had moved into the center of Harlem or Watts. He'd get the feeling the brothers don't want him there and the minute he let his guard down, the worst of them would cut his throat."

Chapter Four

Behold...A Pale Horse

As the warring factions in Somalia remained deadlocked in their peace negotiations for the ninth straight day in Addis Ababa, Ethiopia, the United States lost the first of a long list of her sons to die in Somalia. A patrol from the 3rd Battalion, 11th Marines, deployed to Somalia from Twenty-Nine Palms Marine Corps base in California, was fired on by snipers in Mogadishu. After a "fierce firefight," the patrol regrouped and later found the body of PFC Domingo Arroyo of Elizabeth, New Jersey.

The attack was the first open assault on U.S. troops. The attacking Somalian force was described as "a substantial number of Somali gunmen," said Marine Colonel Michael W. Hagee. According to Hagee, the Marines would not change their patrolling policies and, in fact, would intensify their search for arms and guerrillas. Later, U.S. Marines searching a building killed a Somali gunman who threatened them with a heavy machine gun. In one week Marines confiscated sixteen truckloads of arms and ammunition, including 265 rifles and 55 machine guns. Ramona Ortiz, Arroyo's mother, answered government officials' condolences with tear-streaked cheeks and

41

mute grief as rain splattered the window where she kept a U.S. flag.

Four days after Arroyo was killed, Somali civilians led Marines to "a mother lode" of arms and ammunition. More than one thousand tons of arms and ammunition were discovered in bunkers in Mogadishu. At the same time, a firefight erupted near Buur Lego about 65 miles northwest of Mogadishu at night. Approximately a dozen Somali gunmen pulled over a civilian farm truck carrying a family and other passengers, then fired upon an Army patrol that drove up on the scene. The bandits opened fire when the patrol was 30 yards away and eight bullets hit the lead American vehicle. The soldiers, using night vision goggles, returned the fire killing six Somalis and wounding six others. Three of the Somalis who were killed were members of the family on the truck. After the firefight, Captain Tom Wilk, commander of Echo Company, 2nd Battalion, 87th Infantry who led the patrol said, "There was no way you could tell who was a good guy or who was a bad guy." No Americans were wounded or killed in the fighting, and most of the bandits escaped. Still, blood trails led into the bush indicated that several of the bandits had been wounded.

Earlier that day, Marines shot a Somali who pointed a pistol at them. His condition was not determined because, although he fell, the Marines didn't bother to look for him after the incident. Tensions were beginning to ratchet up and in the highly-charged atmosphere of Somalia, death lurked around every corner and became a constant companion.

As the 43rd Engineers and soldiers from the 10th Mountain Division began to penetrate the countryside of Somalia (along with the troops of twenty allied nations), 237 officers and men of the 3rd Battalion, 9th Marine "Shadow Warrior" Regiment departed Mogadishu as the first contingent to return to the

Doorway to Hell

United States. They soon would be followed by another 556 Marines headed back to Camp Pendleton, California. As they were leaving, 440 soldiers were arriving to bolster the Army's Logistics Command.

After having to fight their way past snipers and ambushes consisting of fire from mortars and automatic weapons, the 43rd Engineers, initially moved into Engineer base (a sparse, canvas-covered, tent camp with few amenities) in Mogadishu, and began unpacking their equipment which had been unloaded from the transport ship *Bellatrix*. As they labored under the blast furnace created by an unrelenting sun, they formed their opinions of Somalia and made the inevitable contrast between their current situation and the conditions under which the veterans of the Persian Gulf War operated. One NCO who was a veteran of Vietnam and the Persian Gulf War said, "This place is a nightmare. You can't believe it. If given a choice, I would volunteer for another tour in Vietnam to get out of here." Shortly after fighting his way out of an ambush where he buttstroked a Somalian gunman and relieved him of his clan knife, 1LT Brian Wheeler, signal officer for the 43rd Engineer Combat Battalion echoed the Sergeant's thoughts when he wrote his family on a torn piece of MRE carton (Meals Ready to Eat--sometimes referred to as "Meals Rejected by Ethopians) serving as a makeshift, postage-free, post card..

In fairness, this may have been true during Operation Desert Storm, but the veterans of the six months in the Saudi Arabian desert during Desert Shield, who lived in sand foxholes during the heat of the day and freezing temperatures of the Arabian night, would obviously hold a different view.

As the 43rd moved toward their assigned headquarters at Baidoa, 125 miles west-northwest of Mogadishu, fighting intensified in the capital. Firefights broke out throughout the city and Marine Warrant Officer Gus Axelson was blown off his feet with a Somali bullet through his shoulder. In the same firefight, Marines killed six Somali guerrillas and wounded three others. On the same day, when Belgian paratroopers came under sniper fire, they stormed a building in the port city of Kismayu, killed three Somali gunmen and wounded five others.

Then during a routine patrol near the old university stadium which housed nine hundred men and women of the Marine's 7th Regimental Landing Team, Lance Corporal Anthony Botello of Wilburton, Oklahoma, walked into a burst of fire. He later died on the operating table of the Swedish hospital. U.S. and Oklahoma state flags were lowered to half staff throughout his home state by order of the Governor. In Oklahoma's rural Latimer County, all flags were lowered to reflect a special grief by the residents. Virtually all of them knew the former Marine as the tailback for the Wilburton High School football team just a few years before, but few, if any, realized why he died.

In the midst of the fighting in Mogadishu, many of the Americans became cynical about the whole operation. Soldiers and Marines in Mogadishu proper didn't see any starving people. Sacks of grain and food labeled "USA-NOT FOR SALE" was being sold on the streets of Mogadishu's Black Market.

Staff Sergeant Sylvia LeMay said, "It's all wasted. If the people who donated this and the money to getting this stuff over here could only see where its actually going: being sold to get money to buy more guns. You see Somalians selling food out of bags that say 'Donated by Nebraska.' Its not getting to the people who need it. I hate to sound so negative about it. I was positive when I came here.

"The main problem is the breakdown in the system. The rice and stuff comes in and you could have trucks drive it out to the villages, but they don't. They have Somalians do it. Then their

Somali buddies buy it and sell it back to their own people for profit. If we're going to let them deliver it and have control like that, then we're spinning our wheels."

Complicating the frustration was that although the soldiers saw little starvation in Mogadishu, they saw plenty of disease and weapons, things they could do nothing about. According to policy and regulations, they were prohibited from using medical supplies to treat Somalians unless the condition was caused by American troops. Specialist Fourth Class Adam Woodill, a member of LeMay's platoon said, "We can feed them, but if their jaw is busted and they can't eat, then we can't do anything about it. It doesn't make sense."

This was in direct contrast to "lessons learned in Vietnam" wherein U.S. military units made great efforts to go into villages to treat the sick and injured to create and reinforce a positive feeling toward the American presence. It came under the heading of "Winning Hearts and Minds," and in the majority of cases, worked well--as long as the "pacified" village was not abandoned to Vietcong occupation later.

American field units in Somalia knew how to do the job, but were prohibited by political policy derived from the United Nations--who had no experienced people from the Vietnam theatre of action. This was complicated by the Clinton administration's lack of experience or knowledge of the mistakes made during the Vietnam war because they had virtually no military experience to draw from, either tactically or strategically.

Woodill saw children and adults with open, infected sores, malformed limbs and skin diseases. The tremendous medical needs of the Somalians and the soldiers' inability to do anything about them, either because the needs were beyond their skills or authority, drained his morale and those of the other soldiers and Marines in Mogadishu.

LeMay added, "It makes you feel helpless when you see these people and they're all shot to hell, and there's a truck that's all shot to hell, and all you can do is patch them up and put them on their way. When we try to confiscate drivers' weapons at a roadblock, the drivers are often so frightened of traveling without protection, they refuse to go any further."

Woodill commented sarcastically, "If you like Peace-Corps type humanitarian service missions with the potential to have to be 'robocop' in combat, if you can be that type of dual schizo personality, then this is great."

Other things didn't make sense to Woodill either. He went on, "It sounds weird, but I wish I could see up north to Baidoa," he said, "I actually would like to see a village full of starving people, just once, and then help feed them and feel like I'm doing something."

What Woodill wished for, the engineers of the 43rd experienced.

When LTC Larry Davis' engineers moved out of Mogadishu they encountered armed Somali gunmen and where forced into sporadic combat all along the route. When they arrived at Baidoa, they found an "austere city that we could smell before we saw it." The 1st Battalion, Royal Australian Light Infantry Regiment provided security around the city and periodically became engaged in firefights with gunmen in the area. Although U.S. Marines, French Foreign Legion, and Australian Light Infantry had preceded the 43rd Engineers, many of the dead had already been buried and the airfield was secured. As noted by the battalion Operations Officer, Major Allen C. Estes, "When we arrived at Baidoa, I was surprised it was so calm. Time magazine had indicated that it was a boneyard. I was expecting to see a lot of starving people. The Australians were already in place at the airfield, and they were running patrols in the city itself and would regularly become engaged in firefights. Because Baidoa itself was so dangerous, all friendly traffic was routed around the city."

Upon arriving, the 43rd set up its headquarters at the Baidoa airport. After establishing its command and control center, LTC Davis dispatched elements of the Battalion to surrounding towns with the primary mission of rebuilding the road network for food could be deliveries by truck convoys. The objective of the operation was to get food to the outlying areas, and this meant road construction. The engineers were now in their element.

Charlie Company was assigned to Task Force Durham in Jiliib named after LTC Dwight Durham, Executive Officer of the 36th Group who commanded the Task Force.. With the battalion's Headquarters and Headquarters Company (HHC) based at Baidoa, the rest of the battalion was assigned to other basecamps. Alpha Company's mission was to rebuild the road network from Baidoa to Wajiid to Oddur, which was fundamentally the sector held by the French Marines and Foreign Legion. Bravo Company was assigned to the road network between Bardera and Baidoa. Charlie Company would work the road from Marka to Jiliib. Each company worked in two different directions simultaneously, thereby maximizing their roadbuilding capabilities.

One of greatest challenges faced by the Engineers was maintaining the ability to communicate over so wide an area. Only a few weeks before they departed Fort Benning the Battalion was issued ICOM SINCGARS (Integrated Comsec Module Single Channel Ground-Airborne Radio Systems) and technical manuals. 1LT Brian Wheeler, the 43rd's Signal Officer, had only that limited time frame to familiarize himself and train his commo people on the use of the system before the unit's deployment. When they arrived, the SINCGARS system was placed in full operation, which made the 43rd one of the first units to successfully deploy the Army's newest radio system in a combat zone. At the same time, they were also using Vietnam-era. obsolete AM radios to supplement the SINCGARS system. However, the Battalion didn't have enough other communications equipment to maintain normal FM, AM, and telephone nets, and was forced to borrow what they needed from the 10th Mountain Division.

Additionally, because Wheeler and his communications chief, Sergeant First Class Osieo Lopez[9] had to set up retransmission sites, the two men were forced to travel in Humvees by themselves between the cities in which the 43rd had units. In the process, they saw the devastation that covered the country. As they installed OE-254 long-range antennas to provide connecting linkage between radio systems among the 43rd's scattered units which were consistently running into ambushes, they came in contact with the residents of the smaller Somalian villages throughout the outback from the Ethiopian border to the coast.[10]

During one such trip, they sighted a high mesa off the road. In the generally flat desert of western Somalia, any kind of rise in the terrain was an anomaly. Because the height of the mesa would enhance reception from one transmission site to another or to a receiving station, they dismounted from their Humvee and laboriously climbed to the top of the several stories high tabletop mesa. As they clawed their way to the top, they were overcome with the smell of death. Covered with sand and sweat, they crawled over the edge and walked onto the flat, sunbaked roof of the mesa.

Doorway to Hell

What they discovered shocked them with an image neither would ever forget. It was a scene out of Hell.

They had stumbled into an entire village of Somalians which had been slaughtered by warlord gunmen from an adjoining clan.. Not a single man, woman, or child had been left alive. Some of the skeletons and rotting corpses clearly showed signs of mutilation and torture, with many of the bodies having been hacked into parts by machetes. They would later discover that this was not an unusual occurance, and indeed was a common practice between many clans.

Later, in the process of entering the outlying villages, the two soldiers who were traveling alone because the Australians had just enough troops to protect the Battalion's engineers and the Baidoa airport, they met numerous Somalian residents in the desert outback.. They made a point to pay appropriate respects to the village "Shirs" or elders as men of worth and dignity. Lopez and Wheeler could recognize the "Shirs" by virtue of the expertly carved walking staffs they carried which served as a badge of authority and office. Many of them served in the capacity equivalent to American mayors and judges.

The Americans were prohibited from sharing any of their food with the Somalis because of their state of malnutrition, the highly concentrated MREs (Meals Ready To Eat), according to American medical officers, would devastate their digestive systems.[11]

Having nothing else with which to repay the two Americans for the respect the Americans bestowed upon them, the village elders would reveal where the land mines were located in the road ahead. In one village, the elders told the signal team where there were gunmen waiting in ambush on the road leading to their destination.

Doorway to Hell

Since the FM radios had only a 35-kilometer range, the signalmen set up double retransmission stations between Baidoa and Wajiid. One team one-third of the way out from a transmitting station received messages on one SINCGARS frequency. It then re-transmitted the message on another frequency to the second team which was sitting in the middle of the desert two-thirds of the way. The second team would automatically retransmit the message on still another frequency to Wajiid. As a result, the 43rd's signal personnel set up one of the Army's first double retransmission site operations in a hostile fire environment for the newly-developed SINCGARS system as well as tactical/satellite, AM/FM, commercial satellite, mobile subscriber switches, digital group multiplexing equipment and wire. In the process, however, the signal teams traveled over more of southern Somalia than did anybody other than the battalion commander and some of his top key personnel, such as the battalion's Command Sergeant Major. In the process though, the signalmen were on their own and were forced to fight their way out of several ambushes in which they became engaged.

Next to the Battalion Commander, the battalion's Command Sergeant Major (CSM) is often among the most powerful and influential individuals in a battalion. As the top non-commissioned officer, the CSM was a "Shir" among "shirs," and the top NCOs of the 43rd, especially the company First Sergeants (HSC; 1SG Robert R. Lightfoot, Jr., A Company; 1SG William S. Spencer, B Company; 1SG David Whitten, and C Company; 1SG Romey Green III), were acutely aware of his status.

In the course of carrying out his duties, Command Sergeant Major Lawrence Maxwell inspected his troops in Bardera, Oddur, Wajiid, and Jiliib. Describing the cities his troops went to, he said, "Wajiid looked like something out of a National Geographic magazine covering prehistoric life. The people were reasonably content and were surrounded by herds of animals. It was tough on the troops because our engineers were camped near a dirt road, and the dust was knee deep and as fine as talcum powder that caked itself on uniforms, equipment and even in nasal cavities.. It penetrated everything including air filters on our equipment. It was only through the ingenuity of our personnel that we kept our vehicles and generators running. Oddur was in the middle of nowhere. It reminded me of a French colonial base camp with courtyard squares and a sense of regimentation. It had the appearance of a city in India under British colonial rule.

"Jiliib was in a lowland area with poor drainage and all of the animals, insects, and misery that goes with that kind of terrain. The place had been a battlefield during the recent war between Somalia and Ethiopia and was loaded with buried land mines. Jiliib was also the place where our troops found dens of deadly black mamba snakes.

"By far, the worst was Bardera. Although the city had hard-stand buildings, the smell of death was everywhere. The old Italian village which was a refugee camp outside of the city was a nightmare. Everywhere you went, the ground was covered with the dead and dying. Vomit from the sick and human feces from diarrhea patients covered the ground. Soldiers were ordered to immediately wash their hands if they touched a Somali." Then he added unashamedly, "I wasn't the only one who wore a scarf over my face which was the only way we had to filter the stench in the air."

For the rest of their lives, Bardera will remain in the memory and nightmares of the American officers and troops who served there. The Battalion's Chaplain, Captain Dale Forrester of

Doorway to Hell

Allejo, California, previously a United States Navy submariner prior to joining the Army as a Chaplain, described his reaction to the Italian Village, the worst area of Bardera,

"I'm not quite sure why they call it an Italian village. I've been told that way back when the Italians colonized Somalia the confusion that resulted from the clash of two cultures produced these temporary settlements outside the village walls. I guess you could call it a slum, a stick-slum outside a village of mud and stick and straw and dirt-floor huts.

"I visited Bardera's Italian Village. First, I smelled it. It was sweetly putrid. Then I saw the mounds: scores of stone-covered mounds. These are the too shallow graves of the victims of famine, civil war, and a culture that values a camel more than a woman or child. Some of the graves were freshly dug. New victims arrived every day. Remote villages had still not received food and bandits stole food that they did have so the people made miles-long treks to Italian Villages where there is hope.

"The Italian Village swarmed with women and children, thousands of them, seemingly all begging for food or water or clothing or cooking pots or anything that would separate them from the occupants of those shallow, stone-covered mounds. Women held out the edges of time-worn rags in silent entreaty for a piece of colored cloth to cover their near-nakedness. Children begged for anything and everything. Most remarkable in this most remarkable place: they begged for ballpoint pens. School was in session and a student needs a pen.

"I visited the orphanage there in the Village. I met Abdul Mohammed. Abdul was about fourteen or fifteen. No one knows for sure. Birthdays aren't a big event when living until tomorrow takes up all your time. Abdul had walked for days from his village to the Italian village. He hadn't eaten since God knows when. He is about five feet tall and weighs maybe fifty

52

pounds. Abdul was so thin you could almost see his spine through his stomach. When the Marines first met Abdul he was so weak he couldn't stand. When I met him only three days later, Abdul could stand and walk if only with the faltering steps reserved for the aged. Abdul is alive. He had food. He has a rag for cover. And, he has hope.

"I never knew her name. She stood naked, alone on toothpick legs by a dirt-floored, mud and stick and thatched-roof hut in the orphanage. She could have been thirteen or fourteen but she hadn't entered puberty yet. Perhaps her body was refusing to be used to bring another life into a place where there is almost no life at all. Her face was expressionless as she looked at the strangers escorting food convoys and bringing gifts to the women and children of the Italian Village. Her hands weren't stretched out in eager anticipation of the good things that Americans bring. It was as if nothing good had come her way and never would.

"I had a camera with me, but I couldn't photograph her misery. It was too private, too personal to be shared through the impersonality (*sic*) of a camera. I could only see it with my heart and weep. She had no dreams to dream. Should she survive, her future is mutilation at puberty, and then serving as a beast of burden as one of her husband's wives.

"The Marines beat swords into plowshares. They built a playground in the Italian Village. Two Soviet-built antiaircraft gun platforms have been turned into merry-go-rounds. Sounds of gunfire were replaced with squeals of joy.

"Bardera's Italian Village is Somalia. It is a paradox of hope and despair, a mixture of good and evil, humanity at its best and at its worst. The Village elders said we can try, we can help. Our help won't help everyone, our trying will fall short, our work isn't perfect. But we made a difference. And that is enough."

Doorway to Hell

The impressions other troops formed were reflections of their own experiences.

Sergeant Geraldine Broh of Shirley, Massachusetts was an Army Reservist serving with the 711th Adjutant General Company (Postal). She was one of 50 reservists assigned to the postal company and attached to the 10th Mountain Division to provide mail services for United States military personnel and American civilian workers during Operation Restore Hope. When she first arrived in Somalia, she found the country "gorgeous and desolate." But, the further she traveled from Mogadishu, the more she saw the starvation that racked the country.

She reported, "It was sad to watch mothers carrying their nearly starved children in wheelbarrows to a UN hospital." Yet in the middle of attempting to help the Somalis, violence was a constant neighbor. Broh was riding in the back of a 2 ½ ton truck headed from Marka to Mogadishu to pick up newly-arrived infantrymen and mail when a firefight erupted on the rural road. Several armed Somali bandits ambushed the truck from the side of the road. Broh grabbed her M-16 rifle and returned the fire, killing one of the bandits. As a sergeant, assisted by some of the troops in the truck, she helped capture three other ambushers.

While the soldiers in-country fought Somali snipers, insects, disease, mines, and ambushes, the UN effort itself came under fire. A report for the Center for Strategic International Studies in Washington D.C. concluded, "The UN has a lot of structural difficulties in trying to coordinate military action, which is why it hasn't been too successful." The report went on further to point out that the U.S. Joint Chiefs of Staff's directorate for strategic plans and policy was already assessing future U.S. involvement in UN operations. It recommended establishing a

54

joint planning group for military operations at the United
Nations, planning groups for UN related activities on the staffs
of the U.S. regional commanders, a high technology
communications unit for the UN for military operations and
rejuvenation of the UN Military Staff Committee.

The report also emphasized the fact that the lack of U.S.
involvement in UN peacekeeping operations as in what was the
former Yugoslavia would prolong conflicts because only the
United States "possesses the military forces needed to
accomplish the task."

William Durch, senior associate at the Henry L. Stimson
Center in Washington, and a specialist on UN peacekeeping
issues said, "We are often the nation that has to take the first
step." Durch added, "A clear distinction must be maintained
between peacekeeping missions like those being carried out in
Cambodia, and more traditional military operations like the
Persian Gulf War because each requires vastly different forces,
equipment and planning needs."

A key difficulty with the concepts advocated was that no
clear definition of "peacekeeping" existed. The fundamental
definition kept changing. The obvious question that the troops
on the ground were asking was how do you keep the peace if
peace doesn't exist in the first place?

In the past, the term referred to soldiers patrolling within a
demilitarized zone while the opponents negotiated. In Somalia,
there was no "zone," very little negotiation, and a great deal of
violence.

What the troops in Somalia were participating in without
realizing it was what would eventually become known as "Peace
Making,"--or at least a pioneering version thereof.

Chapter Five

Liberation of the Outback

On January 22, military spokesmen in Mogadishu announced, "Some American troops the United States had hoped to pull out of Somalia before, or soon after President Clinton's inauguration, could remain until March. No timetable could be set until the UN Security Council adopts a resolution necessary to transfer control of the U.S.-led relief operation to a UN peacekeeping force."

While Chaplain Forrester was recording his impressions of the Italian village of Bardera, Robert Oakley was accusing the United Nations of "dragging its feet" in taking over military command in Somalia from the United States. Meanwhile, due to the necessity of establishing some form of native police force, the U.S. extended its original mission of providing security and distributing food and began training and equipping a police force in Mogadishu. Oakley said that military commanders decided to act because of the potential for continuing Marine casualties as a result of the vacuum created by the lack of a local security force. Oakley publicly questioned if the U.S. was being "sucked in deeper" than it originally intended.

Meanwhile, soldiers from the 10th Mountain Division swept the city of Afgoi for arms. Afgoi was important because it sat astride a crossroads which would serve as an important link in the shipment of food from the Mogadishu docks to the countryside. When the soldiers arrived, the air was heavy with the smell of manure and thick with the aroma of warm, moist earth. The sweep turned up thirteen rifles but demonstrated that U.S. Forces could enter any place they chose to go. Afgoi citizens told the Americans that the city had fifty "bad men" who were armed but who fled into the countryside when the Americans entered the city.

While the soldiers of the 10th patrolled Afgoi, the 43rd's Engineers were penetrating the desert-like countryside with their bulldozers, trucks, and road graders. LTC Davis' troops had already begun constructing more than eight hundred miles of road network, a 1500-man base camp at Bardera, a headquarters base camp at Baidoa, partial base camps at Wajiid and Oddur, built a Bailey bridge and upgraded the base camp at Marka. Using huge bulldozers and other heavy equipment, Davis' Engineers tore into the existing donkey-cart trails and roadbeds four inches deep, then leveled, packed, and widened the road surface. The equipment was followed by a parade of Somali children who hungrily scrounged through anything the Engineers discarded, such as MRE cartons and garbage.

In the heat that ranged from 100 to 120 degrees with humidity topping 70 percent, Davis was forced to stand down his personnel at the height of the afternoon to prevent heat exhaustion and heat stroke. Command Sergeant Major Maxwell ensured that all troops consumed adequate amounts of water to avoid dehydration and remained in full uniform to prevent sunburn. In equatorial Somalia the sun has the capacity to blister unprotected skin in a fraction of the time it takes at Fort Benning., officer who commanded the

"Task Force Durham" was sent to the isolated town of Jiliib and was comprised of "C" Company of the 43rd, commanded by Captain John G. Reilly, a tall, lumberjack-built Irish-American, and the 63rd Combat Support Equipment Company, from Fort Benning. Both units rebuilt the road between Jiliib, the southern Somalian city of Marka, and the port of Kismayu to the south of Mogadishu. This project was accomplished in two weeks. They also repaired Jiliib's street system where, according to Durham, "potholes were large enough to lose a 2-1/2 ton truck." Within days, local farmers began bringing into Jiliib's marketplaces bananas, mangos, sorghum, and grain.

The area south of Jiliib, unlike the more parched areas of Somalia where the 36th's Engineers had been assigned, lies in a green area of the Jubba River valley. Cattle in the valley are fat and lazy, well-fed warthogs regularly gather around watering holes, and camel herds graze near hundred-acre sorghum farms. Baboons play in the trees, and an occasional lion (who wouldn't mind feasting on a baboon lunch) was seen by the troops of Task Force Durham.

The Somalis in the countryside near Jiliib were much better off than their countrymen further north. There was food available from the area, and as soon as the road networks were improved the farmers of the Jubba River valley could deliver their products to market for sale. In fact, one of the greatest concerns of the Somalis who lived there was that baboons would steal into town and carry away a couple of human babies every year. The area, however, was deceptive. While "Task

Force Durham" was there, they had not only mines to deal with on the road and in surrounding areas but also cobras and black mamba snakes. All soldiers were warned by Command Sergeant Major Maxwell and the company First Sergeants to shake out their boots and uniforms in the morning when they awoke. Few had to be told twice.

Durham pushed his task force in Jiliib toward Bardera, 334 kilometers to the north. Meanwhile, the 642nd Combat Support Equipment Company from the 10th Mountain Division, part of Task Force-43, began pushing south. The new two-lane road was built six miles east of the old road to avoid flooding from the Jubba River. Durham, however, was faced with a different problem. Before his Engineers could proceed toward Bardera, they had to clear their way through 10-12 kilometers of a minefield left over from some old battle between clans. Unfortunately for Durham's men, there were no records kept and none of the local Somalis knew where the mines were. In the process, one Italian-made, plastic mine detonated beneath an armor-plated, mine clearing bulldozer. The bulldozer was temporarily knocked out of commission. The 63rd also discovered a large cache of Soviet-made unexploded mines, artillery shells, and mortar rounds which had to be disposed of before road construction began.

The process of building the roads provided all members of Colonel Anderson's 36th Engineer Group with an insight into the contrast between a modern and a virtual Bronze-Age society. The Engineers' giant earthmoving machines, bulldozers, and graders sometimes had to move over to accommodate nomad camel caravans loaded with a tribe's entire complement of possessions as they ambled by on their way to a new home site. The soldiers stared in disbelief as Somali men would get into shoving matches over the ownership of a plastic water jug that Americans would routinely discard when empty. Sergeant David Hubert commented that what surprised him was the fact that the Somalis built little mud-covered, stick-woven huts while perfectly serviceable concrete housing was nearby. However, they were obeying the orders of the local warlords who ordered them to remain in their huts, or they would be shot.

While the engineers worked on the roads, helicopters had to carry the burden of transporting food and troops. In a country of 248,000 square miles, there were only 1,700 miles of paved, all-weather highway. The rest of the ground transportation network consisted of camel paths and unimproved roads that led to washed out bridges. The constant high temperatures, humidity, and swirling fine dust played hell with the helicopters. The red, talcum powder-like dust was sucked into air cleaners, oil filters, and carburetors, requiring an accelerated maintenance program. To keep their rifles and machine guns from jamming, soldiers and Marines stretched condoms over their muzzles--one lesson remembered from Vietnam--and additionally wrapped water soaked neckerchiefs around their receivers to keep out the fine dust.

Soldiers had to use bulldozers to clear brush from runways, but in doing so, tore up the topsoil. As a result, any kind of aircraft created an enormous dust problem that created visual brownouts over an airstrip. To avoid sitting on the ground any longer than necessary, pilots would conduct engine checks once they were airborne.

Wooden shipping pallets were spread in an attempt to keep the dust down. At Baledogle, AM2 metal matting was used to extend the eastern end of the taxiway on the crude airfield.. They also used road oil to coat the runway to keep the fragile powder from being sucked into the computerized equipment on board the aircraft. (Such a procedure if performed in the states would've resulted in a massive EPA fine for polluting the ground.) Maintenance on aircraft, due to the demands of flying in such an inhospitable area, increased 20-40 percent. Every ten flying hours, the crews had to wash out the engines with water and with chemical solutions every 30 flying hours. Furthermore, the crews were forced to use precious decontaminated fresh water for the job. Somali water was so polluted that engines would clog from the impurities.

An idea that developed during the Persian Gulf War was used with great success in Somalia. Portable clamshell aircraft hangars were used to protect helicopters once they were on the ground. Made of vinyl and stretched over aluminum beams and sealed against outside wind and dust, they operated in the same manner as a clamshell, opening at one end and closing like a clam. The temperature inside such hangers was always 20 degrees cooler than it was outside.

Spare parts became a problem for the helicopter fleet. Although they arrived in-country with a basic load, due to the demands placed upon the equipment, a system was set up with Signal personnel to place satellite calls to Aviation and Troop Command headquartered at St. Louis, and a new replacement part would be in Somalia within six days. Still, the demands for maintenance and repair parts was considerable. The Army began to study the concept of storing aviation parts at strategic places, much as it did with tanks and tank parts in Saudi Arabia after the Persian Gulf War, or pre-packaging them for shipment with each aviation unit. As one pilot said,"What good is it to be able to fly a helicopter 200 miles per hour if you can't get it started?"

Other challenges were more subtle. Another limiting factor was the language. American military police at Baledogle had no Somali-speaking personnel, and soldiers had to muddle through their issued Somali-language handbooks to make themselves understood. The commander of the MP unit based there considered hiring local interpreters despite the risk of acquiring somebody who had an ax to grind. Colonel Sandy Weand, who was deployed to Somalia from St. Louis, said, "You never really know if an interpreter has his own agenda. You don't know what they are interpreting for you. Everybody is suspicious of everybody else here and everyone is part of a clan or a political organization."

While the pilots of LTC Gary Coleman's task force from the German-based U.S. V Corps, who flew 30 Blackhawk helicopters out of the former Soviet-built MiG fighter base, and the MPs supporting them were trying to fly, communicate and establish order at Baledogle, other commands had more serious problems. In Mogadishu, riots and fighting erupted between clansmen. Marines attempted to separate the factions, but the fighting turned fierce and bloody in short order. Then, in the mistaken belief that U.S. Marines killed six Somalis, the mobs turned on the Americans, stoned them, and set discarded tires on fire. The riots erupted one day after a Marine killed a thirteen-year old Somali who ran toward a Marine vehicle carrying a package. It was the first overt public demonstration against U.S. forces.

Other things were changing in Somalia as well.

Prior to the revolution, a Somali man could buy a bride for one hundred camels if the woman's family agreed to the dowry. With the disruption of the country, lack of security, constant threat of gunmen, and the death of so many Somali women leaving fewer potential wives, the price for a fourteen-year-old bride had increased to one hundred camels and a Russian-made AK-47 rifle.

While the Engineers put up with the dust of Wajiid, the 400,000 mines planted in the country during the war between

Doorway to Hell

Somalia and Ethiopia, black mamba snakes in Jiliib, and the horror of the Italian village of Bardera, Robert Oakley had become a "peer among peers." A career foreign service officer, the sixty-one-year-old Oakley had been brought out of retirement to broker a truce in Somalia. As former ambassador to Somalia, his role became that of a proconsul among the warlords. In a country where power is the only source of respect, Oakley commanded more power than anyone. The Somalian warlords went to great pains to praise him, but Oakley knew that it was based on nothing more than the fact that he had more guns and troops than they commanded. Quartered in the former Consolidated Oil Company compound in Mogadishu, referred to as "New Villa Somalia", he said, "I want to avoid the mistakes we made in Vietnam where we created structures and they were artificial. And when we left, they collapsed."

"U.S. officials in South Vietnam," he recalled, "largely wrote that country's constitution, recruited and anointed its presidents, and built up a national army that was never given primary responsibility for combating the Communist insurgency." He said, "The lesson for Somalia, is that Somalis themselves must take the lead in rebuilding their own country and forming new structures of government and society. The United States must be here only as a catalyst to bring the various groups and factions together." Oakley's description of the U.S. role exceeded the original mission and mandate which was to alleviate the starvation. There was no qualifying statement contained in the U.S. objective to bring various groups and factions together.

However, the paradox for Oakley was that the more he injected himself into the process as a catalyst, the more indispensable he became. In the absence of any identifiable and neutral leaders commanding the respect of Somali warlords, and with the United Nations largely discredited among the Somalis,

Oakley filled the vacuum. As a result, Somalis came to view him as the linchpin of the country's reconstruction and reconciliation.

An American southerner, Oakley didn't hesitate to use analogies from the American Civil War to prove his point. When reporters, U.S. Congressmen, and others complained that Somali clan leaders weren't reconciling fast enough, Oakley pointed out that it took generations for Americans to reconcile after Appomattox. He said, "In comparison, the Somali clans are moving at the speed of light."

Other problems, however, plagued the allied effort from the lowest to the highest levels. While CNN reporters beamed sound bites back to the United States in real time, because of inter-service lack of coordinated communications and compatibility in equipment, U.S. military medical personnel in country could not communicate with their naval colleagues on hospital ships offshore. Often wounded would arrive by helicopter with no advance warning of the condition for which the naval doctors should prepare.

Command and control of what became UNOSOM (United Nations Operation Somalia) II, flowed from the Secretariat of the United Nations to the military commander. The United States had contributed about 3,100 combat troops to that force. This element, which was only a fraction of the total of U.S. troops in Somalia remaining under U.S. command, had been placed under OPCON (OPerational CONtrol) of UNOSOM II. This meant that the UN command directed their operational activities. Although all other command functions involving pay, discipline, and promotion were retained in the U.S. chain of command, U.S. troops were placed under operational control of LTG Cevik Bir of Turkey. Having Bir in command of UNOSOM II addressed Washington's concerns about placing U.S. troops under a foreign command plus simultaneously relieving the Arab nations' anxieties about having a Muslim oversee the relief effort. The compromise was reached because Turkey, although a Muslim nation, was a member of NATO.

It should have come as no surprise that such a quagmire of command would exist. To understand the predicament that was becoming apparent, an understanding of exactly what the United Nations is necessary. The UN was created in 1945 by representatives of Russia, France, and other World War II allies.

The resultant UN charter was never voted upon by any country's population, but was accepted by many governments as a solution to the problems that led us into two world wars. Yet even as the Cold War proved that even member nations would fear each other and would not get cooperation, no one seemed to note the fact that the UN had its own agenda and would make up the rules as they went along. Korea was an early example.

When US forces in Korea deployed on operations, whether on the ground or in the air, they were almost always opposed by a superior force that seemed to be waiting for them as if they had access to their tactical plans.

That is because they did.

All plans for operations of UN forces had to be cleared by the UN headquarters. The secretary in charge of clearing these plans was always a Soviet general! The Russian would then advise the Chinese and North Koreans of the upcoming operation, location, time and unit strength, and the Communists would prepare accordingly. It was not until long after the Korean war that the American population became aware of the behind the scenes machinations that cost thousands of American lives.

Still working toward its standing as the world government in which nations were rapidly becoming subservient to it, the

Doorway to Hell

UN in Somalia and elsewhere continued to stomp around like an elephant in a mine field. It placed US troops under the command of foreign officers, which destroyed proper chain of command functions, training, and espirit d'corps, not to mention command and control problems, equipment differences, and poor coordination between units and lack of any coherent value system. It was still an issue the UN commanders would demand again and again–until maybe someday mix-matching troops and nationalities might work.

With the announcement that the largest bulk of American troops expected to withdraw by April, and at the latest by May 1993, coalition forces took over larger roles in the operation. The Italian Army's 187th Parachute Regiment, by itself, stormed Gailalassi to put an end to ongoing warfare between clan members. Because that area of Somalia had been ruled by Italy for eighty years prior to the 1960 independence of Somalia, many Somalians spoke Italian. The paratroopers were successful in bringing peace to the town without casualties on either side.

Other Italian forces raided a residential area in northeast Mogadishu at the same time, finding weapons hidden under bags of rice, blankets, and furniture. The cache included 25 rifles, 22 heavy weapons, 103 hand grenades, 12,000 electronic detonators, 26 artillery and mortar shells, two TOW and two MILAN missiles, and four rocket-propelled grenades.

American soldiers and Marines rapidly became leery and on edge around Somalians. One battalion command sergeant major who had been a PFC in the Mekong Delta and in the Central Highlands in Vietnam said, "It's the Nam' all over again. We're here to give help to a people half of whom want us desperately to get the Hell out, and the other half want us desperately to get the Hell out after we give them all of our money and kill the other half."

When Americans went on patrol and dismounted from their vehicles for short foot patrols, they stopped speaking to the residents, many of whom were children who would gather around the Americans whenever they saw them. One British correspondent noted that the uniforms were different but "it might as well have been Belfast." Somalian gunmen unhesitatingly used women and children as shields to keep U.S. troops from firing on them as they threatened the Americans. But women and children were also dangerous. With the threat of women and children bearing unwelcome gifts which they could deposit into a Humvee with the fuze burning, or being in the sights of snipers as they made their way on the streets, the soldiers began to suspect everyone. As one said, "It ain't paranoia if we're surrounded by real enemies."

Yet the lack of communication complicated the situation. As one American patrol returned to their vehicles, dozens of children and a sprinkling of adults gathered around and clapped and chanted in unison, "Galeano satowala...Galeono satowala." The Americans immediately went on alert. They thought the children were yelling, "Death to the imperialistic swine" or some other epithet. The Somalian children were really singing "Good Friends, Welcome."

The "peacekeeping" mission had placed the U.S. troops in a purgatory between combat operations and keeping the peace. In the absence of support from U.S. or UN civilian agencies, light infantrymen from the 10th Mountain Division and Marines from the lst Marine Division were forced to negotiate with civilian Somalian leaders and oversee the establishment of local authorities and a police force, while protecting supplies from the very people with whom they were negotiating.

Doorway to Hell

"This is the worst kind of warfare," LTC Jim Sikes, commander of the 2d Battalion, 87th Infantry said, "because it is insidious. You are surrounded by the enemy. You are surrounded by friendlies. You are surrounded by the innocent and the guilty."

CSM Hubert Key, the top NCO in Sikes' battalion echoed his thoughts with the comment, "We're not trained in civil affairs. Our training teaches us, if the enemy's in front of you, destroy him."

Even Major General Steven Arnold, commanding general of the 10th Mountain pointed out, "It's uncharted waters. We've never had to deal with something this complex."

"Complex" was an understated choice of words if there ever was one to describe the situation in Somalia. Confronted by increasing evidence that the disaster in Somalia was caused by the Somalians themselves, U.S. troops became increasingly cynical. LTC Sikes said, "There are only crooks and the helpless in this country." Another officer was less generous. He said, "The only thing wrong with this country are the people who live in it."

When security around the port at Merca began to tighten, the Somalis began to loot the barges on which food supplies were still stacked. 10th Mountain infantrymen fired in the air to chase them off. Then they discovered a Somali tugboat captain was starting to loot the supplies from the barges he was supposed to guide into port.

One of Sikes' officers openly asked, "Is there one son-of-a-bitch in this town who doesn't loot?" The next day, Captain Gordy Flowers, commander of Alfa Company of Sikes' battalion reported that looters had paddled out to a barge the previous night, found it empty, so they stripped it of wooden planks instead. Commented Specialist Fourth Class George Crowder of Headquarters Company, "This is a nation of kleptomaniacs."

Theft by Somalis frustrated the Americans enormously. In Baledogle, in a compound that was supposed to be secured by Moroccan soldiers, items began to disappear from the area. Among the missing items was one American soldier's hand-held portable radio. When 1SG John Thompson, 984th MP Company from Fort Carson, Colorado who was attached to the 2d Brigade, 10th Mountain, looked up, he saw a Somali boy "standing there grinning. He took off after him but the kid was too quick, and the boy never stopped grinning."

In another incident, a soldier's M-16 rifle was stolen from a mess tent, reported the commander of the 984th, CPT Carson Mayo. The rifle was later recovered after investigators interviewed some Somalis who told them where the rifle could be found. In another instance, a 9mm Beretta pistol was stolen from the holster of a senior U.S. Army commander. After extensive effort to locate it, it was quietly "bought" back from Somalis who claimed to be in contact with the thief.

It was possibly accumulated frustration with the ineffectiveness of the Moroccan troops and the diligence of the Somali thieves that caused a soldier from the 10th Mountain Division's 602d Maintenance Company to fire several rounds after he spotted a Somali inside the compound before morning light. No one was hurt and because the Rules of Engagement might have been violated, the soldier and the incident were immediately placed under investigation.

The Rules of Engagement were imposed by diplomats working with desk-bound brass who didn't face the dangers of the Somalian operation on the streets and in the outback. In Mogadishu where sniper fire was a daily occurrence, stealing was rampant. One female guard in a convoy between the

Doorway to Hell

American embassy that served as the Headquarters for U.S. forces in Somalia, was hit in the head by a Somali man and had her sunglasses ripped off her face as she held an M-16 rifle. Since she could not use deadly force against the assault, she began carrying an MP truncheon in addition to her M-16. She could use the truncheon to defend herself when the use of her rifle might result in her court martial.

The same situation existed all over the country and was exacerbated by the unwillingness of the allied high command to disarm the Somali population. For example, once in Marka, the 10th's infantrymen were faced with a quandary. The high command including General Hoar, commander of CENTCOM, concurred that to disarm the bandits whose actions brought the allies to Somalia in the first place was impractical. Even after entering the city, troops had to tiptoe around the issue of disarmament. Although LTC Sikes gave the locals a timetable under which "Technicals" and crew-served weapons were banned, the tight rules of engagement made any enforcement of such a rule unrealistic. Sikes pointed out, "The rules of engagement do not permit searching private homes. They allow use of deadly force only to protect lives and sensitive items such as weapons and night vision goggles, not to accomplish the mission of securing food supplies." MG Arnold, in supporting the policy said, "Disarmament isn't the mission; reduction of arms where we're operating is part of the mission." Yet paradoxically he added, " to disarm the Somalis is impossible."

By not disarming the Somali population, U.S. forces only postponed the inevitable by putting off dealing with the bandits until they were fired upon by them. In the meantime, convoys continued to be ambushed, snipers continued to test U.S. resolve and reactions, and soldiers on patrol in Merca knew they were sitting ducks for any young Somali with an AK-47 who wanted to ingratiate himself to the local warlord.

Being unable to separate the good from the bad made it even more confusing. 1LT Roger Harvey, Scout Platoon Leader in Sikes' battalion reported that his men, while on patrol, received considerable help from locals who led them to arms caches and depositories of looted rice. However, when the arms caches were in private homes, Harvey was prohibited from entering the homes to retrieve the arms or looted rice due to the Rules of Engagement. This did little to enhance the stature of U.S. troops in the eyes of Somalis who wanted to cooperate. If Somalia itself was hard to understand, the polyglot of UN forces made it even worse.

However, other UN contingents did not have their hands tied as tightly as the American troops. The London Telegraph reported that a Belgian unit caught a young Somali thief and then roasted him over an open fire as an example to others. The resulting court martial gave the two paratroopers who committed the act a month in jail and a fine of 200 pounds.

In another instance, a Belgian soldier forced a young Somali to drink salt water, eat pork (which will send a Moslem to Hell), and then eat his own vomit. Another Belgian NCO was accused of murdering a Somali whom he was photographed urinating upon, and another child who was caught stealing food from the paratroopers, died after being locked up in a metal storage locker for more than two days.

The Belgians were not the only troops caught abusing civilians. The Canadian Parachute Regiment was eventually disbanded after the public was made aware of a videotape taken by one of the paratroopers showing paratroopers torturing a juvenile Somali to death for stealing. This issue went all the way to the Canadian parliament who voted to disband the entire regiment for the actions of a few troopers. This would be akin to disbanding the Americal Division for the actions of one company at the My Lai massacre during the Vietnam War.

In Milan, gruesome photos were published in a magazine of Italian paratrooper torturing a Somali boy and raping a Somali girl. In one instance, a young Somali girl was tied to the front of an armored personnel carrier and raped while officers looked on.

The *South China Morning Post* reported that an Italian battalion commander had sexually assaulted, then strangeled a 13-year-old Somali boy. And in 1993, the same publication charged that Italian soldiers beat seven suspected Somali thieves, killing one and beat to death a 14-year-old boy who sold a false medal to them. When asked about this, an Italian paratrooper said "What's the big deal? They are just a bunch of Niggers anyway."

The above examples illustrate that sending soldiers into a civilian arena to serve as policemen is not conducive to good public relations, much less peace making or peace keeping.

By February lst, no less than twenty-one countries had provided troops as part of the multi-national operation to secure relief supplies and keep the peace. The nations participating ranged from token commitments from Nigeria which initially committed only two soldiers, to sizeable troop contingents from longtime U.S. allies. Unfortunately, troops were needed so desperately that no consideration was given to the past history of Somalia or how Somalians would react to the presence of certain nations on their soil.

Furthermore, each nation had its own agenda and its own interpretation of what it had agreed to do with its troops. One example of such national latitude manifested itself when the l0th Mountain Division met the Italians.

Doorway to Hell

The Italians had previously occupied large portions of Somalia and had promised 3,000 troops. By Christmas, 1992 only 80 had arrived.

A meeting was called in Mogadishu where the Italians announced that they intended to command an aid convoy to Jalaaqsi, 140 kilometers north of the capital. LTC James Sikes' troops of the 2d Battalion, 87th Infantry were to be detailed to provide security for the convoy. The meeting was to firm up arrangements and coordination between the two forces.

Sikes was told initially the convoy would involve fifty food trucks. At the meeting however, the Italians revised the number downward to "perhaps four or five trucks." Furthermore, they left the impression that in their view the convoy didn't need any food at all.

Sikes replied, "I really think we need to have some food on the convoy." The l0th Mountain Division battalion commander couldn't see any point in running a convoy through hostile territory to a starving town without any food resupplies, to a population who hated the Italians.

The Italians got Sikes' point because three days later the infantry battalion commander received word that the Italians had canceled the convoy for lack of food. However, the opinion among U.S. officers involved in the aborted operation was that the Italians were far more concerned with "planting their flag" in Jalaaqsi, than with delivering food to starving Somalis.

A similar situation developed on December 31st when the 2d Battalion of the 10th Mountain's 87th Infantry Regiment deployed to the coastal town of Merka. Major Martin Stanton, operations officer for the battalion expected to link up with a convoy escorted by Italian troops. The rendezvous was scheduled for 0930 hours.

The Italians didn't get around to leaving Mogadishu until

1230 hours, forcing Stanton to leave a small and vulnerable contact party at the checkpoint to wait for them.

The Italian contingent eventually arrived nearly half a day late, spent ten minutes greeting the waiting U.S. troops, and promptly returned to the relative safety of their compound in Mogadishu. The food was destined for the town of Qoryooley, 20 kilometers northwest of Merca, but the Italians were so unpopular there the local Somalis insisted that U.S. forces deliver the food. One member of the 2/87th commented, "Now I know how the Germans must have felt with the Italians as their allies in World War II."

The 10th Mountain Division's other deployed battalion to Somalia, the 3d of the 14th Infantry, encountered similar problems in the southern port of Kismayu. A U.S. patrol from the battalion heard rapid-fire gunshots and reported over the radio they were taking fire. A half hour of confusion followed before it was determined that Belgian paratroopers were amusing themselves shooting monkeys.

One senior NCO and former Vietnam veteran bluntly referred to the Belgian paratroopers as a "uniformed and armed mob of undisciplined white trash." The Belgians got the message quickly that the American troops were singularly unimpressed. Belgian protests were lodged with the 10th Mountain Division for the rudeness of troops in that command. The division's commander, Major General Arnold, had to pull out his diplomatic hat and say, "I have the utmost respect and admiration for many of the allied armies around the world. While we do things differently, there are many nations that can do peacekeeping, and do it very, very well." MG Arnold obviously didn't know of the Belgians ongoing crimes against humanity.

Doorway to Hell

Unfortunately, there was no standard definition of "peacekeeping" so whatever soldiers did "well," qualified under that category. That statement salved the hurt feelings of the Belgians, but it didn't do much for the troops under his own command.

Semantics were replacing reality and the mad hatters were out in force.

While Arnold was trying to smooth over the hurt feelings of offended allied soldiers who were frankly told by their American counterparts that they were "undisciplined shitheads,"[12] Colonel Philip Anderson's Engineers in the "outback" were at the end of the allied supply line. As a result, the contrast of living conditions between the soldiers of the Persian Gulf war and those in Somalia was stark.

Mail was late if it arrived at all, and when it was delivered it came in batches. Personal care packages from home were also difficult to get because of the overloaded Army postal system in Frankfurt, Germany and the small number of military postal personnel committed to Somalia. Initially, with no access to telephones other than for emergencies and with a poorly supported postal system, the troops in-country "might as well have been in space as in Africa," said some. "It's like we don't exist," said SFC Katherine Harry with the 984th Military Police Company.

The lack of mail wasn't the only reason the soldiers felt abandoned. Print media representatives would occasionally go into the outback with a convoy but broadcast teams found operations in-country to be extremely difficult, dangerous and expensive because of the lack of any electricity or tele-communications infrastructure. As a result, video news coverage was largely confined to Mogadishu.

"The lack of broadcast news coverage and the lack of "any soldier" mail[13] left the feeling by many of the troops that they were cut off. And for the soldiers who served during the Persian Gulf War who remembered being able to literally walk up to a telephone booth set up in the desert behind their units on the Iraqi border and call home," the contrast was heartbreaking and stark. The troops in the outback felt as if they were on the surface of the moon..

Sergeant Gustar Cunningham pointed out that lack of communication with his wife who was expecting a child in five months, has "been the most frustrating aspect of Operation Restore Hope, even worse than the relentless heat or the fine red sand that permeates all aspects of life." The Sergeant, a combat medic in Headquarters and Headquarters Company, 10th Aviation Brigade, 10th Mountain, echoed the feelings of others in his unit.

Living conditions for the troops in the outback were harsh at best. There was no entertainment other than what the troops created for themselves. During the height of the heat of the day when LTC Davis found it necessary to shut down his engineer construction operations to avoid heat prostration and heat strokes, his men--and women--would take photographs of one another,[14] run cockroach races,[15] and play cards under the shade of canvas covers while sweat wilted the cards because it was too hot to sleep in what would instantly become sweat-soaked cots.

Two years before, the infrastructure for the Persian Gulf War was so well coordinated and supported that some soldiers rode into combat in leased Toyota four-wheelers with air conditioning. Salad bars in Riyadh were better than civilian ones in Columbus, Georgia, and Post Exchange facilities took on the appearance of fully-stocked department stores.

Doorway to Hell

In Somalia, the closest thing Colonel Philip Anderson's Engineers had to an air-conditioned Toyota was a "CucV" which amounted to a stripped-down, camouflage-painted, Chevrolet Blazer, and T-rations (prepared meals packaged on trays, and usually heated before being eaten), and air conditioning consisted of opening the windows.

For the Engineers in the "outback," there was no convenient PX or store at which they could buy a candy bar or comb. A resupply run over the Somalian countryside from Jiliib to Mogadishu was a distance of two-hundred miles. The trip took six to eight hours one way and had to be accompanied by armed vehicles for security against ambushes which regularly occurred as the convoys passed from the boundaries of one clan into another. Additionally, travel over the outback's road networks battered the vehicles and often suspensions and springs would have to be replaced after one trip. Anderson's engineers were virtually isolated.

Colonel Anderson was not the type to wait until bureaucracy straightened itself out. So he "supplemented it" by sending Chief Warrant Officer Pedro Arroyo to Nairobi and Mombasa, Kenya to purchase bulldozer parts and other equipment the Engineers needed.

Anderson's Engineers were in-country for twenty-one days before they received a visit from the Marine Corps Base Exchange based in Mogadishu. Many of the Army engineers had already run out of personal items such as shaving gear, soap, deodorant, and toothpaste. By the end of three weeks in the Somalian outback, the Marine Corps was perceived by the troops of the 36th as a reluctant ally at best.

Major Mark Feierstein, 36th Group S-4 (logistics and supply officer) shared their opinion when he said: "I'd describe the Marines' degree of support as 60 percent non-cooperation, and

77

40 percent cooperation." However, Feierstein had more problems than merely the relations between the Army and the Marine Corps.

The Army had its own internal problems as well. Feierstein tried to come up with 100,000 gallons of bottled water but could contract for only 50,000 gallons. Until a resupply could be obtained, water had to be prioritized so the Engineers were reduced to "whorehouse"[16] baths, performed with a rag and a bucket of water, until they eventually received an Australian shower which is a bucket of water emptied into a canvas bag with a spigot on it and hung from a tripod of poles..

The Engineers had brought with them enough MRE's and T-Rations to last only three weeks since the plans indicated that they would be resupplied well within that time frame. Unfortunately, for twenty of the twenty-one days, the Engineers had chicken for their one hot meal per day. Albeit there was a variety including chicken cacciatore, chicken ala king, and chicken breast, Feierstein blamed, "Some lazy SOB at some Army depot other than Fort Benning, just drove his front-end loader up to one rack of shelves and scooped up hundreds of tray packs of chicken destined for the troops in Somalia, instead of taking different varieties of meals from different shelves."

While Feierstein and his supply personnel were trying to straighten out logistical nightmares for troops used to the best of everything in the most devastated country on earth and 200 miles away from any support, Somali gunmen had long before set aside their fear of coalition forces and began testing the perimeters and security zones.

Australian soldiers killed one Somali and wounded two in a firefight at a Mogadishu bridge, and the Headquarters of the 43rd U.S. Army Engineer Battalion and Royal Australian Light Infantry Regiment that provided security at the Baidoa airport was almost simultaneously involved in a similar attack by Somali snipers. Three Australians were wounded in the Mogadishu battle, the first casualties suffered by the Australian Army since Vietnam. At the same time, a mob of protesters gathered in Mogadishu and began to stone Canadian troops. Firing began and one Somali was killed and two were wounded.

Fighting erupted throughout the country simultaneously. While traveling between Baidoa and Washid, the 43rd's signal team consisting of 1LT Wheeler, SGC Lopez and a driver were ambushed. They emptied their M-16 magazines at the gunmen and left several Somalian gunmen dead on the desert. But because they would have to "account" for the spent ammo under the restrictive Rules of Engagement in effect at the time, they traded some fresh batteries to the Australians for replacement ammunition and said nothing about the firefight.

However, progress was made despite the clan gunmen using coalition forces for sniper targets. Children led American Marines to a huge cache of weapons and equipment being used as playground equipment. The cache included six surface-to-air, forty-foot Soviet-built rockets and launchers in concrete bunkers. Although the missiles were damaged, four of their warheads were still live and active.

On Sunday, February 21st, a group of officers from LTC Davis' 43rd Engineer Battalion staff visited the Baidoa orphanage which was run by Irish Concern, a humanitarian organization. During the visit, 1LT Wheeler met Valerie Place, an Irish Concern Volunteer, who took him on a tour of the facility. Since Wheeler had previously visited Ireland, the two hit it off and they spent four hours together. During the tour, they met one tiny boy who had just arrived. The boy was emaciated from starvation, dehydration, and disease. He looked up at the 6'5", two-hundred pound American officer with awe. Then, he saw a ballpoint pen in the Lieutenant's hand and his eyes brightened. Wheeler knelt down and gave the boy the pen since the children were short on all sorts of school supplies. The boy repaid Wheeler with a wide smile, possibly the first one he had managed since he had arrived at the Baidoa orphanage, because a pen was valued by all Somali children to use in school, and especially one from an American officer. Wheeler then said goodbye to Valerie Place and the boy, and returned to his headquarters at the Baidoa airfield.

In the afternoon of the next day, Wheeler was monitoring the battalion's radio nets and overheard a report that an Irish Concern truck convoy from Afgoi to Baidoa was ambushed outside of Afgoi. Three members of Irish Concern were shot by Somali gunmen. A passing military unit called in Medevac helicopters and the wounded were evacuated to a hospital in Mogadishu. He later learned that Valerie Place was one of the casualties. She had been shot in the head several times at close range and died on an operating table in Mogadishu. With haunting thoughts of the young Irish girl, he felt compelled to visit the orphanage to see how the boy was coming along. Upon arriving he couldn't find him. The lieutenant stopped another orphanage volunteer and asked about the boy. The volunteer told him that the boy died the night before from starvation. They buried him still clutching a ballpoint pen. It would be months before Wheeler would be able to shake the nightmare of the Irish girl and the Somalian boy.

Within hours of the raid on the Irish Concern convoy, Kismayu exploded with clan fighting that resulted in the deaths of more than two dozen Somalis. The three thousand American troops stationed there, although scheduled to pull out, were ordered to postpone their withdrawal. As a result of the fighting, Robert Oakley and General Johnston sent an ultimatum to

General Mohammed Said Hersi Morgan. He was to pull his troops out of the city immediately and relocate them outside of Derba, fifty miles northwest of Kismayu. Failure to do so would result in his forces being "engaged."

Morgan maintained that his followers acted without his consent or knowledge. Oakley and Johnston replied: "There can be no excuse or pardon for the well-planned actions of your forces and senior commanders in attacking Kismayu."

Protests erupted overnight in Mogadishu, led by General Mohammed Farah Aidid who accused the U.S. of backing Morgan. Chaos erupted as rock-throwing and tire-burning crowds roamed the downtown areas of Mogadishu and shut down all relief efforts. Mobs quickly formed and hundreds of screaming Somali youths hurled rocks, lumber, and garbage at allied tanks, armored personnel carriers, and personnel in central Mogadishu.

Attackers threw two grenades into one compound and wounded a Marine in the hip, while another Marine went down with a bullet in the leg. The mob assaulted the Egyptian embassy and looted it, then tried to overrun the French embassy. But French Foreign Legionnaires, who had been sent to Somalia from French Djibouti, fired into the air and drove back the rioters. American-led forces, finally having their fill of these blatant assaults, rolled out Pakistani army tanks and used heavy weapons on the Mogadishu gunmen leading the riot, ending it.

The eight hours of battle marked the worst fighting that had occurred since the allied coalition arrived on December 9th. Machine gun and rocket fire echoed across the capital of Somalia as the UN considered evacuating the relief agencies and aid workers. U.S., Nigerian, and Botswanan troops launched a three-pronged attack on two areas of the city that had previously proven to be centers of sniper activity. The forces finally established order by midnight.

However, the fighting continued again the next day, and U.S. Marines and Nigerian troops found themselves under fire, with one Nigerian soldier wounded. A Battalion of Marines, covered by Cobra helicopter gunships, conducted a house-by-house search for weapons, and found four machine guns, three rocket-propelled grenade rounds, one 60mm mortar, four rifles, and a "load" of ammunition.

Heavy fighting broke out around the former Conoco Oil Company compound which had been serving as a makeshift U.S. embassy and as the headquarters for the United Nations forces in Somalia, and sniper fire continued within two miles of the downtown center of Mogadishu. The fighting undercut United Nations plans to take over the peacekeeping role from the Americans who were expected to stabilize Somalia before Boutros-Ghali's United Nations troops could assume command.

On March 1 the same warning that was given to General Morgan was provided to Colonel Jess. Jess was ordered to move his troops eighty miles north of Kismayu. The order was futile. Colonel Jess's and General Morgan's militia were already battling one another in Kismayu. Two Somalis were killed in the clan fighting, and Belgian paratroopers killed a third when he tried to throw a grenade at them. On the same night Australian troops were engaged in a firefight at Baidoa and killed one Somali gunman. Aid workers and political analysts blamed General Mohammed Farah Aidid as the main obstacle to peace since he had approximately ten thousand well-armed clan gunmen at his command. When the fighting finally subsided, ten Somalis were dead in Kismayu. During the clash, U.S. Army Special Forces Sergeant First Class Robert H. Deeks of Littleton, Colorado, was in a Humvee that hit a land mine ninety miles northwest of Belet Huen. He became the third American to lose his life in Somalia due to hostile action. A Purple Heart would be presented to Deeks' family.

During the same day, Private John D. Robertson, Tustin, California, swerved to avoid a Somali pedestrian and overturned his wrecking truck. He was crushed and died immediately. His family would not be eligible to receive a purple heart from the Secretary of the Army since he lost his life under "non-hostile" conditions.

Chapter Six

Declare Success And Get The Hell Out

On March 2, Robert Oakley declared that the U.S. mission was a success and that it was ready to turn over the Somalian operation to the United Nations. At peace talks in Mogadishu fifteen clans turned in lists of their weapons as the first step toward disarmament. The next step would be to determine a date for them to gather for further negotiations.

Ironically, the apparent success of the U.S. forces created a euphoria in the United Nations. The success achieved by U.S. troops in Somalia contrasted with the quagmire that had developed in the Balkans. Among growing domestic sentiment for the U.S. to intercede in the Balkans to end the fighting and horror stories of concentration camps, ethnic cleansing, widespread rape, genocide, and indiscriminate attacks on civilians, a long voice of caution and experience was heard. Marine Corps Lt.Gen. Martin Brandtner, director of operations for the Joint Chiefs of Staff said Defense Department officials examined options including providing security for relief convoys, establishing feeding sites, and disarming warring factions. In each case, he pointed out that such options would represent an "enormous pool that would drain resources." He added, "I would submit that no matter what you do, you have to have a force able to fight." By making such an argument, he effectively laid down the gauntlet to those who advocated involvement of the Americans, because to field a force to fight meant that a fight and casualties were likely. In an era when the Persian Gulf War created the impression that a victory can be achieved on the cheap, body bags would not be acceptable.

While the politicians and the brass complimented themselves over the U.S. success in Somalia, and debated about whether or not to intercede in the Balkans; U.S. Marine Gunnery Sergeant Harry Conde, a radar technician based at Twenty-Nine Palms, California, was appearing before the first pre-trial hearing on charges that he used "excessive force" when he wounded a seventeen-year-old Somali who tried to steal his sunglasses. While Conde was riding in a convoy, he shot the boy when the Somali reached into his Humvee and grabbed Conde's glasses. At the same time, a pre-trial hearing was held for Marine Sergeant Walter Andrew Johnson who killed a thirteen-year-old Somali boy who rushed toward his vehicle carrying a package. Two other boys were wounded when Johnson, who was manning a machine gun, opened fire on them. The pre-trial hearings were held to determine if the men should be court-martialed.

Conde testified, claiming self defense, "Some people want us here, some people don't. When you're out there, you can't tell. How many times in Vietnam did kids carry explosives into villages? We were approaching a turn, the next thing I know, something covers my face and all I feel is my head going back.

It was an instinct, just a reaction. It was my intent to repel hostilities."

While Conde was testifying, a Marine patrol was fired upon by Somali teenagers in the Hammer Jadiidi district of Mogadishu. Three Somalis were killed and two wounded, including one armed thirteen-year old. Hammer Jadiidi residents reported that young looters entered the market area and opened fire on vendors when they resisted. The Marine patrol was nearby and returned the fire.

On Tuesday, March 9, U.S. Marine guards killed a Somali who crawled over the wall of the former university complex that served as the headquarters of the coalition. The two Marines involved in the shooting claimed that the Somali had stopped and appeared to be drawing a weapon. That shooting, too, would be investigated and subject to a pre-trial hearing and possible court martial. While the Marines conducted their hearings, U.S. troops began to leave Somalia.

One of the commands that departed was the 36th Engineer Group minus the 63rd Combat Support Equipment Company, a vertical construction platoon from the 43rd Engineer Combat Battalion (Heavy), and the 608th Ordnance Company. The Engineers had done a remarkable job in record time, rebuilding more than eight hundred miles of road network throughout southern Somalia. Because they did, food was now flowing into the "outback" and life was already beginning to take on the appearance of normalcy.

Nobody would suspect it at the time, but the homecoming for the returning 43d Engineers to Fort Benning was held in the same rusting, dilapidated, WW II hanger at Lawson Army Airfield that the battalion would enter nine months later on their second homecoming from Somalia. After arriving, the one hundred replacements that had been assigned to the 43rd to achieve full strength for Somalia returned to their home bases as far away as Fort Lewis, Washington, and Fort Hood, Texas. They took with them the personal appreciation of the Battalion commander. There was little else he could give them. Nobody in the Pentagon had authorized issue of any special medals for service in Somalia as they quickly did two years before in the Persian Gulf. Not even the Southwest Asian campaign medal was authorized, despite the fact that Somalia was virtually adjacent to the Arabian peninsula.

Robert Oakley was right.

The mission as originally articulated by President Bush and the United Nations had been a success. The armed forces of the United States had done its job and surviving Somalians had been saved from starvation. The U.S. forces and their allies had taken Somalia a long distance, and now it was up to the United Nations to broker a peace out of what limited order had been restored.

The small contingent of American troops who were still left in Somalia agreed with Oakley. The American troops who remained were frustrated because the job they had been sent in to do had been accomplished. Many wondered why they had been left behind.

In the midst of that frustration and lack of purpose, morale and discipline began to suffer. It was during this period that SSG Anthony Varga, a telecommunications NCO with the U.S. 516th Signal Company, 86th Signal Battalion, 11th Signal Brigade was charged with participating in the torture of two Somalis using a hand-cranked field telephone generator to shock them because they were suspected of stealing a tape recorder and other items from an Army truck. Varga was convicted by the Courts Martial panel but the conviction was later overturned.[17]

Even when good order and discipline was under control, the lack of apparent purpose affected the perspectives of the rest. One Marine sniper, Lance Corporal Ryan McBride, of Villa Park, Illinois, summed up the feelings of many other Marines when he said, "It's already a waste of time. People throw rocks at us and constantly test our discipline with threatening language and behavior, and we can't shoot them. We came halfway around the world to help them out, and if they don't care why should I? Our job is done, it's time to go home."

What McBride and the rest of the U.S. force didn't realize was that they were about to become victims of "mission creep," a gradual shift in the original purpose and mission for being in Somalia.

The critical problem was that nobody in the White House, Congress or the Pentagon saw it coming either despite the more than clear signals given earlier by Boutros Boutros-Ghali. He, however, could see the handwriting on the wall. The American military, which he desperately wanted to control, or at least have unlimited access, was not allowing itself to become his private army. The U.S. would unilaterally withdraw if the UN did not get its act together. So, Boutros-Ghali announced at a meeting in Addis Ababa, Ethiopia, that the United Nations needed $166 million[18] for the remainder of the year and even more importantly a wider mandate for rebuilding the war-torn country. With such a mandate Boutros-Ghali would have the leverage to convince the Americans to participate. Even if they didn't, with additional funding, he could use the money to pay the troops of Third World nations to occupy Somalia and to provide the military force necessary to carry out UN objectives, whatever they were.

President Clinton was aware that Secretary of State Warren Christopher[19] was negotiating with Boutros-Ghali to draft a plan replacing American soldiers with a UN multinational force. Since American troops were returning rather than deploying, Clinton left the detail work to Christopher and other subordinates, concerning himself with the proposed national domestic health plan on which he was focused. By March, in a hurry to withdraw most of its troops, the U.S. agreed to a UN Security Council resolution specifying what the United Nations would do to "rebuild Somalia" with UN troops maintaining security. Under the UN plan, southwestern Somalia was to be divided into nine humanitarian relief sectors, each the responsibility of a different country.

Australia, Belgium, Canada, France, Italy, and Morocco assumed responsibility for large sectors. The U.S. Army would be responsible for Merca and U.S. Marines would have two sectors including Mogadishu and an area on the Kenyan border including Bardera.

If there was a definitive, critical change in the mission for U.S. troops still in Somalia, the Security Council's resolution must be considered the point on which it turned.

"Operation Restore Hope" on which the whole operation was initiated, became "Operation Continue Hope" because it was now obvious that "Operation Restore Hope" had ended. "Mission creep" had taken over and instead of relieving starvation, "nation-building" was the new objective.

That complex and time-consuming mandate should have set off alarm bells somewhere in Washington because such a mission was open-ended and ill-defined. However, Somalia was "not on the front burner" since other events in the world at the time were occupying the government's attention. Furthermore, U.S. forces in Somalia had already been reduced from 28,000 to 4,700, and because things were going so well, no warning was sounded. This failure was compounded by the fact that it was widely known throughout the administration that the President wanted foreign affairs to be handled by Secretary of State Warren Christopher.

Intensifying the effect, the U.S. Senate on a voice vote and with 32 co-sponsors, passed Senate Resolution 45 on February 4, 1993, endorsing the nation-building mission and favoring the use of American troops to support it, for several years if necessary. The Senate's resolution was sent to the U.S. House of Representatives which passed it 243-179 on May 25, 1993. The Senate resolution was passed at the same time that President Clinton removed most remaining U.S. troops as President Bush had intended. Nobody had the foresight to see the ramifications of what dangers such endorsements would create.

In the process, 4,700 American troops were left in Somalia, and command of the overall operation was handed over to the UN. Had Clinton pulled out all American troops at this point, events that were to follow in Somalia would not have involved American forces. The joint Congressional resolution provided, among other considerations, "specific statutory authorization for the use of U.S. troops under the War Powers Resolution." It also stated that such authorization would be terminated in either twelve months or expiration of the mandate of the UN-led force in Somalia, whichever came first. The resolution, almost as an afterthought, also commended "the armed forces for successfully establishing a secure environment for the humanitarian relief operations in Somalia."

General Mohammed Farah Aidid may have been regarded by some as little more than a brutal African warlord, but those who knew him well also knew that he was extremely intelligent, wily, and strategic in his thought processes. Aidid concluded that since the U.S. and UN were making so much progress putting together the beginnings of a peaceful regime, his chance of eventually taking over the whole country was slipping away. He could retrieve it only by causing enough trouble to disrupt the mission. Furthermore, he was acutely aware that he could order his troops to kill Americans but U.S. soldiers were not allowed to kill him because of the limiting mandate of the UN Security Council[20]. So, in early June he unleashed his guerrilla forces and ambushed Pakistani troops inspecting unguarded weapons depots.

The ambush killed twenty-four Pakistani soldiers.

An outraged UN Security Council responded with a resolution to "arrest and detain for prosecution, trial and punishment" those responsible. Eleven days later, retired U.S. Admiral Jonathan Howe, Boutros Ghali's chief deputy in Somalia, ordered posters plastered on the bombed-out buildings of Mogadishu offering a $25,000 reward for information leading to Aidid's capture.

Allied troops were ordered to attack and destroy Mohammed Farah Aidid's militia and weapons caches. On June 12, U.S. AC-130H Spectre gunships fired the first blasts in what became a major operation to eliminate Aidid's combat power. Beginning at 0400 hours, Spectre gunships backed by UN and U.S. Quick Reaction Forces on the ground, engaged five of the warlord's key facilities, including weapons sites, radio stations, and an abandoned cigarette factory that was the battleground for the June 5 ambush. The attack which lasted over a five-day period destroyed a large number of Somalian tanks and Technicals.

U.S. troops secured one weapons site and one radio retransmission facility. Pakistani troops destroyed the broadcasting equipment at Aidid's Radio Mogadishu, and French

91

Foreign Legionnaires relieved the U.S. soldiers at the retransmission site.

The offensive continued through June 13th, when a few minutes after midnight, a flight of heavily-armed AC-130 Spectres attacked a suspected weapons cache near Aidid's residence, a compound that contained ammunition and Technicals. The Spectres destroyed hundreds of rounds of 105mm howitzer and 40mm cannon rounds, setting off explosions shook the ground and that lit up the sky of the entire city.

Later the same day, Somali supporters of Aidid demontrated at a traffic circle identified on allied maps as K-4. The intersection was manned by Pakistani troops who were individually angry over the loss of twenty-four of their fellow soldiers. Suddenly shots were fired from the direction of the crowd at the Pakistanis. From behind their defensive positions, the Pakistanis returned fire on the crowd of protestors, killing fourteen Somalis. Among the dead were women and children.

The firefight at K-4 created the effect Aidid's guerrilla leadership desired. It resulted in an international incident and undercut the UN's credibility as a stabilizing force in the ravaged city.

Within hours, on June 14th, Spectre gunships hit the compound of Osman Atto, Aidid's chief financial backer, disintegrating it in secondary explosions as stockpiles of ammunition ignited. During the same morning, Cobra attack helicopters destroyed multiple rocket launchers near Aidid's compound.

On June 15th and 16th, Moroccan and Italian troops sealed off the perimeter of a portion of southwest Mogadishu. Pakistani infantry was sent through the area on a search and destroy mission. French Foreign Legionnaires were kept in

92

reserve to reinforce the Pakistanis if they ran into heavy resistance.

The Moroccans moved quickly into position and set up their armored cars thirty meters apart. As the Pakistanis began their sweep, pressure developed on the Moroccans, which in turn began to push back the Somali people who were advancing on their position. They then fired into the air.

Tear gas grenades were thrown into the crowd, which pushed the protesters back from the Moroccans. But as the crowd fell back, snipers opened fire from three sides. The Moroccans began to return the fire. During the firefight, the Moroccan regimental commander was killed when a Somali-fired recoilless rifle shell slammed into his command vehicle.

The French Foreign Legionnaires were committed to secure "21 October Road" which lay on the western border of the city and north of Aidid's compound. The French were ordered to reinforce the Moroccans, but by the time the order arrived, the Legionnaires were heavily committed. Guerrillas had taken a position on the top floors of an old military academy building and had brought the French under heavy fire. The Legion battalion commander was forced to leave three tanks and a platoon of mechanized infantry to cover his rear, as he pulled his troops out to support the Moroccans.

As the French Legionnaires moved toward the Moroccan position, they encountered three separate roadblocks. Taking fire from surrounding buildings, it forced them to deploy their Legionnaire infantry while the tanks crushed the roadblocks. The French finally fought their way through, reached the Moroccans, and began to draw fire away from the besieged position. When the firing began to die away, the Legionnaires dismounted from their armored vehicles to sweep through the area adjacent to the Moroccan position. The house-to-house sweep took two hours to cover a two-kilometer section of the city.

The operation reached a climax on June 17 when UN forces, backed by American Spectre gunships and Cobra attack helicopters, and assisted by the U.S. Quick Reaction Force based on the 22d Infantry, 10th Mountain, swept through Aidid's personal residence and seized a number of weapons sites in the capital city of Mogadishu. The end result of the offensive was that Aidid's logistics base was cut, command and control was interdicted, and Radio Aidid was taken out.

It was a different game now. Aidid had been targeted by the UN and the other warlords weren't strong enough to represent a national rallying point. Without a single national personality to weld together the Somali people, Boutros Boutros-Ghali believed that the UN was finally in the position to dictate an outcome. What Boutros-Ghali and the soldiers on the ground believed were contrasts in perception. Colonel Michael Dallas, commander of the U.S. 10th Aviation Brigade asked the obvious question, "What's the end state? Who's going to be the Somali who pulls a coalition government together and keeps it together?"

Colonel Dallas' observation was reflective of the fact that Somalia had taken on all of the characteristics of a quagmire from which it would be difficult for the UN to extricate itself in order to avoid allowing Somalia to return to what it was when UN troops arrived. Of greater significance was the change that had occurred.

The original humanitarian mission had already been expanded to a "nation-building" mission by the United Nations Security Council.

The latest resolution in reaction to the deaths of the Pakistanis had converted UN efforts to save Somalia from starvation and "rebuild the nation" into a mini-war against Aidid. Madeline Albright, Clinton-appointed U.S. Ambassador to the United Nations, stated that "failure to take action (against Aidid) would have signaled to other clan leaders that the UN is not serious." Furthermore, she called those who opposed such military action "advocates of appeasement."

This view changed, in part, because Aidid turned out to be much harder to locate and capture than anyone believed. Admiral Howe decided to use an American Quick Reaction Force for what amounted to search-and-destroy missions, but Aidid slipped away again.

In such an environment, perception becomes as valid as reality. The perception that Somalia represented an ominous example of the "New World Order" did not please many who had seen developments under United Nations mandate.

Criticism against the President was building in the media, and despite the American troop withdrawals, Clinton and his White House staff finally realized that the situation which had been left in the hands of subordinates was growing out of control. A reassessment was initiated on the premise that the operation was too narrowly focused on capturing Aidid. National Security Advisor Anthony Lake told Clinton, on Friday, September 17th, that he was developing options to shift the emphasis more toward a political solution.

This shift began on the next Monday with a tough letter from Secretary of State Warren Christopher to Boutros-Ghali protesting the military emphasis. Christopher called on Boutros Ghali's urging a stepped-up effort to bring about a political settlement among Somali factions only to be told blandly, "We are already doing all that," which Christopher reported verbatim to the President.

Doorway to Hell

Of greater significance, however, was that while Clinton and the White House belatedly tried to reorient the UN toward a political solution instead of trying to capture Aidid, the UN was preparing one last attempt to carry out what were still active orders. The mission would be given to a force of U.S. Army Rangers who would suffer the worst casualties since German Army SS panzer units surrounded U.S. Army Rangers at Anzio in 1944. The military disaster would also generate a major political fallout for the nation's self-styled "domestic" president.

Boutros- Ghali, an Egyptian, personally loathed Somalian Mohammed Farah Aidid and the feeling was mutual. When retired Admiral Howe placed a bounty on Aidid's head in response to the UN Security Council's resolution, Aidid adopted a siege mentality. While U.S. Marines in Mogadishu initiated weapons sweeps, Aidid conserved his weapons by hiding large caches in the countryside and small amounts in homes of his supporters. Hunted as a "criminal," he now infiltrated his large weapons caches back to Mogadishu.

Howe's action, although pleasing to Boutros-Ghali, horrified the Pentagon.

U.S. officers were concerned about the safety of troops still in Somalia and the attitude of the Somali people who were under the influence of Mohammed Farah Aidid. Furthermore, to the rage of UN officials, French and Italian forces were unable, or unwilling, to stop gun smuggling through a cordon meant to surround Mogadishu. One UN official said, "The Italians are playing traffic cops when the arms come down the road." It was obvious neither the French or the Italians wanted to offend the Somali locals and that they were merely there as a military presence, not as police officers.

Boutros-Ghali and Admiral Howe insisted, with supporting resolutions from both the UN Security Council and the U.S.

Congress, that since there were no countermanding orders from President Clinton to U.S. forces, American military forces should hunt for Aidid under direction of the UN. At this point, American officials were informed that other nations with troops in Mogadishu would not participate in the new mission of urban guerrilla warfare. This was not the mission allied nations had sent troops to Somalia to accomplish, and they refused to become involved in offensive operations. Almost at once, Howe called on Washington for help.

In May, Clinton held a ceremony at the White House welcoming soldiers home from Somalia. Wives at Fort Campbell, Kentucky watched the ceremony on television and Army wife Julie Power openly wondered, "Doesn't he know we still have people over there? The White House ceremony made the country think everybody was back. Our guys were just going." Julie Power's husband commanded the 54lst Transportation Company, 10lst Support Group (Corps) at Fort Campbell. She said, "I talk to relatives who aren't in the military and they say `I thought they were all back,'"

Sydney Hickey of the National Military Family Association in Alexandria, Virginia echoed Power's comments, "Our families are asking 'don't they realize our guys are in danger? They're still going in harm's way.'" He further pointed out that families in the association felt forgotten by the military leadership at the Pentagon.

On June 9, Defense Secretary Les Aspin received a request for a team of Delta Force commandos for the purpose of capturing Aidid. Aspin refused the request. Instead, he forwarded it to the British for a detachment of their Special Air Service to perform the mission. The British also declined. They weren't about to be sucked into Somalia.

Doorway to Hell

Aspin was desperate. He was under pressure from a variety of different sources due to events around the world. In view of possible fundamentalist Islamic threats from Iran, military aggression from Iraq, nuclear capabilities in North Korea, the growing Chinese armed forces, and chaos in the former Soviet Union, the former Wisconsin Congressman who had made a political career of criticizing the Pentagon was now in charge. Aspin would have been better advised to have remained in Congress.

His political instincts tended to cause him to teeter between the military and the more anti-military elements of his party and the White House. Although an indefatigable worker, he displayed the tendency to become overly involved in detail at the risk of failing to keep the big picture in perspective. Additionally, those who worked with him saw that one of his weaknesses was an inability to lead. At the head of the one department in the United States government that respected strong and decisive leaders, Aspin's style was that of an individual who sought compromise.

Additionally, instead of filling important positions within the Department of Defense with experienced personnel, like his commander in chief, Bill Clinton, he gave key positions to the young and inexperienced. These were the same people he came to rely upon to track events all over the world and throughout the defense establishment. This was in conjunction with a major downsizing of the military at the same time it was being loaded down with additional missions.

His political instincts to compromise and split differences affected the deployment of troops in combat. Concerned about General Colin Powell's view that American troops should not be committed without backing them up with overwhelming force, Aspin proposed a "limited objectives school" which was far more effective on paper than in reality. Additionally, he had to provide direction for a Pentagon no longer faced with the Soviets as a threat. As a result, reorganization of the Department of Defense created new fiefdoms with each of them battling for new turf.

Aspin was also weak in his approach toward insisting on coordination with other agencies. The lack of coordination hampered the Pentagon in interagency battles. The National Security Council-State Department axis worked to the Pentagon's disadvantage and often caught Aspin off guard.

Warren Christopher for example, unveiled the six principles of the administration's foreign policy. The first time Aspin knew about them was when he heard them announced on television.

In turn, Aspin, possibly taking direction from "a higher authority" at the UN, complicated the already fractious political relationships by initiating unilateral actions without informing any other department. He made the decision to expand the mission of U.S. troops in Somalia with the approval of the Chairman of the Joint Chiefs of Staff, Army General John Shalikashvili, and passed it straight to the White House for approval.

A man who preferred to deal with memoranda than people, Aspin was further hampered with a culture gap. He was constantly faced with the conflict between the Clintonites in the administration who were of the same philosophical generation as the President, and the military which had already carved out a position of tacit opposition to many ideas of Clinton, such as "homosexuals in the military," and mistrusted their own commander-in-chief's capabilities as a military commander. Aspin was a man under siege in Washington D.C. by both his enemies and those who should have been his allies, but the real problem was that he was more effective at being a critical

Congressman than administrator of the Department he criticized so much during his career.

With American forces on the hunt for him as a criminal, Mohammed Farah Aidid issued orders to "Kill Americans."

On August 8, as four MPs drove down a street in Mogadishu, Aidid's militia set off a command-detonated land mine killing all of the vehicle's occupants.

Body bags being sent back from Somalia were enough to send the message to the White House that events in Somalia were getting out of control. To determine what was going wrong, a special team was sent to Mogadishu. The team returned with a critical report of Admiral Howe for "dropping the political ball," but despite this unfavorable report, no further action was taken either by Aspin or the President.

However, Mohammed Aidid wasn't finished..

From this point on, the "Peace Keeping" mission in Somalia would intensify into a full blown guerrilla war--sans political and media recognition. Despite the attacks against his infrastructure, logistics and bases, Aidid kept up the pressure on the UN.

On June 27, Aidid's militia shot and wounded one Pakistani and two American soldiers along 21 October Road. The compound of buildings lining the road was engaged by U.S. aircraft which included six AH-l Cobra attack helicopters, five OH-58D Kiowa scout helicopters and two UH-60 Blackhawk utility helicopters. Before the attack, UN forces used loudspeakers to clear the area. Once the attack was launched, the Cobras fired two TOW missiles, supplemented by 20mm cannon fire. However, as in previous Cobra attacks, some of the TOWs veered away from the intended targets. The UN had received no reports of any Somali injuries although observers noted one Somali being led away and treated.

Doorway to Hell

On June 30, one Pakistani soldier was wounded in an ambush of his patrol in Mogadishu. A week later, two U.S. soldiers were wounded in Mogadishu when gunmen riding in a jeep fired an RPG rocket at their guard post in the southwestern part of the city. Twenty-four hours after that ambush, Aidid's gunmen killed six Somali employees of the UN who were on their way to work for the UN newspaper *Maanta*. Aidid viewed the publication which had a circulation of 20,000 in Mogadishu as a propaganda weapon of the UN. The six bodies were found on 21 October Road.

In response to the murders, UN forces searched for weapons and tightened security to protect the 1,400 Somalis working for the multinational peacekeeping alliance. The UN force confiscated a cache of a dozen light weapons and detained two Somali men suspected of operating a command post for Aidid.

Four weeks later, on July 24, Sergeant Major Patrick Ballogg and Sergeant Michael Bower were wounded when gunmen ambushed the Humvees in which they were traveling. The acceleration of violence in Mogadishu prompted the Italian government to demand that countries with peacekeeping troops in Somalia consult with one another before any military action was taken against Aidid or any other Somalian warlord.

Tensions had been growing between the Italians and the rest of the U.S. force. U.S. and UN spokesmen had been quoted as criticizing the Italian force for clearing all orders from the UN chain of command through Rome before acting on them, and for independently negotiating with Aidid after the UN issued an order for his arrest. On the Italian side, Italian Foreign Minister Beniamino Andreatta sneered, "U.S. commanders in Mogadishu seemed to prefer to use force rather than diplomacy in Somalia."

Aidid's strategy was successful to the degree that it forced UN troops to remain largely bottled up in their compounds. UN officials conceded that they had no control over 400,000 of the city's one million inhabitants. However, U.S. and UN forces did have control over their own troops.

On August 2nd, Specialist Fourth Class James D. Mowris, was found guilty of killing an unarmed Somali in February. He was reduced in rank to PFC, fined $350, confined to Fort Carson, Colorado for three months, and recommended for a letter of reprimand. The previous February, the 27-year old soldier from the 984th Military Police Company was deployed in a weapons search in a village outside the Somali capital when suddenly, without warning, two Somali men bolted from a building and ran into the open. Mowris and three others fired warning shots and gave chase. During the chase, Mowris fired again and killed Ahmed Miri Asir, 18, one of the escaping Somalis. Despite the fact that government witnesses gave conflicting testimony and the bullet was not recovered, which meant it couldn't be tested to see if it was from Mowris' M-16 rifle, the Courts Martial panel convicted Mowris. Additionally, it blamed Mowris' superior officers for failing to instruct soldiers on how to handle uncooperative but unarmed civilians and stated that the facts of the case required broader investigation.[21]

Forty-eight hours later, a soldier and a civilian engineer employed by Houston-based Brown & Root Construction Company were wounded when their truck hit a land mine in Medina, a Mogadishu suburb. After the explosion, Somalis in the vicinity looted the truck and set it on fire. The two wounded men were evacuated to medical aid just before the Somalis swarmed over it. Later on that same day, Somalis attacked three UN locations in Mogadishu, wounding three U.S. soldiers at two sites. The Somali militia fired six mortar rounds at the former U.S. embassy and university compound, wounding in the chest lLT Robert D. Mon, 46th Forward Support Battalion of the U.S. 10th Mountain Division. At the same time, Aidid's guerrillas fired six RPG rockets at nearby Hunter Base. This attack wounded two soldiers. In a third assault, Aidid's snipers brought the airport under fire, but were suppressed by UN troops who immediately opened up on them with all available weapons.

At noon on the next day, three soldiers escorting a fifty vehicle food convoy from Baidoa to Mogadishu were wounded in an ambush at Baledogle. Moroccan soldiers who were providing security for the convoy returned the fire, repelling the ambushers.

Colonel Jim Campbell, the outgoing commander of the Quick Reaction Force said, "Incoming soldiers should expect more violence in the near term. I think they'll experience intermittent harassment and attacks, and the guerrilla-type tactics will continue." Campbell had a realistic appraisal of the situation.

Where Campbell and others like him on the ground in Somalia had a real-world understanding of the conditions under which they were having to operate, the American people were beginning to suspect that the U.S. was being dragged into a sewer lagoon. This suspicion was beginning to manifest itself in the polls of the upcoming off-year, Congressional elections. Attempting to offset such skepticism, U.S. Senator Carl Levin (D-MI), Chairman of the Senate Armed Services Committee's Coalition Defense and Reinforcing Forces Subcommittee declared Somalia to be a dangerous atmosphere "where the challenges are intense. That is never easy, and it carries some risk." He said further, "Several steps need to be taken to make the operation safer and to improve the changes that it and future UN military missions would succeed."

He continued, "Only recently has the UN's peacekeeping department established a 24-hour situation room. It may be shocking, but not very long ago, there was nobody to answer the phone if it rang after hours or on weekends.

"Also," he pointed out, "the troop quality and political will of nations agreeing to take part in UN operations must be measured better. The most modern, well-staffed command center means nothing if the United States and our allies fail to muster the political will, to back up our words with the teeth of real enforcement."

Levin emphasized, "The decision to relieve the Italian force commander after he balked at carrying out an order to conduct military operations that would have strengthened the UN position was right and proper."

Levin's comments did little to dissuade or persuade the American people. On August 9th, using a command detonated mine, Somali guerrillas blew up an American Humvee which killed Sergeant Christopher Hilgert, Specialist Fourth Class Mark Gutting, and Specialist Fourth Class Keith Pearson who were assigned to the 977th Military Police Company from Fort Riley, Kansas. The fourth casualty was Sergeant Ronald Richerson, assigned to the 300th MP Company stationed at Fort Leonard Wood, Missouri. The loss of the four Americans enraged the rest of the American troops in Mogadishu.

Colonel Michael Dallas, new commander of the Quick Reaction Force said the killings, "prompted great anger on the part of about every soldier you talk to."

When the explosion occurred, the media reported that four MPs had been killed, withholding the identifications until the nearest relatives could be notified. At Fort Riley, Kansas, until Jody Pearson and Pauline Hilgert who lived on post were told, all of the wives of the MPs deployed from that installation waited in anxious fear that their husband might have been one of the casualties. Gutting's father was notified at his home in Grand Rapids, Michigan, and Richerson left behind a wife and two sons who were notified in Portage, Indiana.

For the next four consecutive nights, UN troops took fire. This activity was supplemented by an increased use of mortars by the Somali militia, including several attacks on the U.S. embassy compound itself.

On Capitol Hill in Washington, the deaths of the four soldiers provoked calls to reassess the U.S. role in Somalia. Senate Minority Leader Robert Dole (R-KS), said "It may be time for the United States to consider withdrawing."

The Pentagon immediately responded when Navy Captain Mike Doubleday announced, "One thing I want to make clear is that our policy regarding Somalia has not changed. We are firmly committed to staying the course in Somalia. There has been a great deal of success in Somalia on the humanitarian side. Relief efforts have eased the horrible conditions and widespread starvation seen in news reports of 1992." President Clinton vowed that the United States would take "appropriate action" against those responsible for the blast.

In Mogadishu, Admiral Howe announced to the press that Aidid, "is almost surely responsible for the killing of the four Americans."

While press releases were handed out at the Pentagon and the President assured the American public that action would be taken, Aidid wasn't waiting around to find out what Clinton had in mind.

By August 22, six more American soldiers were wounded. Aspin, who was sailing on Lake Beulah in Wisconsin, received word from General Colin Powell about the casualties. He also was told that Admiral Howe requested a battalion of Army

Rangers and a small detachment of Delta Force personnel. This time Aspin approved the request.

The approval of the deployment of Army Rangers amounted to a drastic change in policy. Experienced Washington insiders and military officials could see that the U.S. was pursuing a military path and neglecting diplomatic options. Five days later, after reflecting on what he'd approved, Aspin gave a speech calling for a renewed effort to find a political solution. Secretary of State Warren Christopher agreed, so the administration "developed" a two-track approach which on its face was contradictory. Efforts would still be made to get Aidid, but Christopher would continue to press Boutros-Ghali to bring the factions in Somalia together through the Organization of African Unity. Apparently, the Clinton administration's new "two-track" policy was to "kill Aidid (if he couldn't be captured) and then negotiate with him."

The problem was that Boutros Ghali wasn't playing the same game. According to sources close to him, he had become obsessed with getting Aidid, whom he personally hated, and was not interested in making peace with the Mogadishu warlord. Obviously, a political solution in Somalia was impossible without Aidid's support, yet he was being hunted as a fugitive with a price on his head.

On August 31, American Rangers raided a UN office believed to be used by the Aidid faction. Inside were nine UN employees, who the Rangers bound while destroying their radios. The employees were taken away for questioning because Aidid's militia had been using the same building the same night it was raided. The conclusion on the part of U.S. intelligence was that Aidid's personnel had penetrated the UN operation in Somalia.

Doorway to Hell

Six days later, Somali guerrillas ambushed a Nigerian platoon on its way to support a combined Italian-Nigerian strongpoint that had been surrounded by a rock-throwing mob. In the ensuing firefight, seven Nigerians were killed, seven more were wounded, and one was taken captive by guerrillas. The Nigerian battalion commander openly complained that the Italians stood by during the ambush and did nothing, refusing to fire in defense of the Nigerians.

Twenty-four hours later, on September 7th, fifty U.S. Rangers conducted an air assault into a block-sized compound in Mogadishu, believed to be the command and control center for Aidid. After a series of brief firefights, the Rangers detained seventeen guerrillas. Two guerrillas were wounded in the operation, and two Rangers were slightly wounded and were treated at UN hospital facilities.

Two days after that raid, U.S. and Pakistani troops became engaged in the fiercest battle to date with Somali militia. The gunmen, using heavy, crew-served weapons, fired on three Pakistani tanks, four armored personnel carriers, a bulldozer and about 100 Pakistani soldiers who were clearing roadblocks. The Somali fire was well coordinated and the Pakistanis soon found themselves in a devastating field of overlapping rifle, machine gun, and heavy weapons fire.

U.S. reinforcements arrived and began firing at the Somalis to relieve the Pakistanis, whose tanks engaged the attackers with 90mm rounds and machine guns. American Cobra helicopters joined in support, firing several dozen 2.75mm rockets, supplemented by 20mm cannon fire, to hose down the Somalis.

One Pakistani was killed. Two Americans and two other Pakistanis were wounded. A Somali 90mm recoilless rifle round set one Pakistani tank, an old American-made M-48, on fire.

Doorway to Hell

Somali snipers wounded three U.S. soldiers during a fierce, two-hour firefight in Mogadishu on September 13. The Somalis were located in the Benadir Hospital, and U.S. forces returned fire from one UH-60 Blackhawk helicopter, two AH-1 Cobras and Turkish armored personnel carriers. The guerrillas were "neutralized," but the pure volume of fire injured and killed numerous civilians in "collateral damage."

On September 14, American Rangers seized thirty-one Somalis in an air assault on the adjacent homes of two leading supporters of Ali Mahdi Mohammed, the warlord in command of the northern half of Mogadishu. Within 24 hours of that raid, a U.S. helicopter fired on a vehicle carrying four armed Somalis when it appeared one of the gunmen was about to fire on the helicopter. Two of the Somalis were killed, two wounded and their vehicle was destroyed.

At the same time, two Italian soldiers were killed by a Somali ambush in Mogadishu's port area and a major mortar attack was launched on the UN headquarters which wounded eleven workers. Those wounded included U.S. Army Captain Lee Hansen, an Army budget analyst from Fort Monroe, Virginia; three UN civilian workers, three Somali workers, two Norwegian troops, and two Pakistani troops.

Boutros Boutros-Ghali continued to demand a military victory over Aidid, but Aspin became leery of the increasing commitment and casualties. On September 23 he denied MG Montgomery's request for tanks. The former Wisconsin Congressman and Chairman of the House Armed Services Committee believed it constituted an "escalation of the military" at a time when the UN was supposed to be looking for a political solution.

It was becoming increasingly obvious to insiders that Aspin was in over his head. His own military service consisted of two years in the Army as a systems analyst in the Pentagon during Robert McNamara's era as Secretary of Defense during the Vietnam War. In his previous Congressional capacity, he had served as the powerful Chairman of the House Armed Services Committee and often subjected members of the defense establishment to withering interrogations before his committee. A colleague in Congress described Aspin: "He is detached, not from the issues, but from the people. He has a hard time relating to the average soldier or sailor or airman."

A poor choice by Clinton, Aspin was in charge of the Defense Department and the position was overwhelming him. His style of methodically analyzing problems until events themselves solved the issues conflicted with the more action-oriented military culture of decision making. The homosexual-in-the-military issue became a bitter and divisive political battle that cost him his "honeymoon" period normally granted by the Washington culture to all new appointees, even though he was carrying out a promise Clinton had made in the presidential election to the homosexual and lesbian community.

Additionally, he was also faced with turmoil in Haiti, a growing nuclear threat in North Korea, and a genocidal war between Bosnians and Serbians. In the midst of the variety of challenges, he failed to grasp that the U.S. was being dragged into a bloody conflict in Somalia. MG Thomas Montgomery realized that only heavy weapons would be able to carry out the mission that American forces had been assigned. He immediately notified Aspin that he needed tanks and Bradley armored fighting vehicles, along with a 400-man Ranger force. Aspin approved the deployment of the Rangers to Somalia but denied the request for tanks and Bradley fighting vehicles based on the rationale that such heavy weapons would be too "provocative." His conflicting decisions simply signaled to the military personnel who were assigned to carry out the administration's policies in Somalia that the Secretary of Defense was confused as to what purposes he was supposed to be pursuing.

As 400 American Rangers landed at Mogadishu airport on August 26, speculation ran rampant that U.S. military leaders were planning a strike against Mohammed Aidid. The speculation was in the fact of stories put out by Pentagon representatives who said that the Rangers were deploying "only to give the Army's Quick Reaction Force additional manpower as it attempts to regain control over southern Mogadishu." They emphasized, "These troops shouldn't be viewed as hit teams." According to Pentagon spokeswoman Kathleen DeLaski, the 400 Rangers would comprise a task force anchored on the 3rd Battalion, 75th Ranger Regiment and led by the 3rd Battalion Commander, LTC Danny McKnight.

On the same day that Carol Jones, spokeswoman for the Army's Special Operations command stated that the Rangers are a "special operations force whose specialties include the temporary seizure of vital objectives and strikes against key enemy military/political personnel." Accompanying handouts pointed out that the Rangers rarely perform regular light infantry missions for long periods, although they are capable of doing so *if properly augmented by other combined arms elements.* Said one officer who had been in-country for a lengthy period of time, "I find it rather odd that they'd send the Rangers in and then declare that they're not after Aidid."

Despite news reports that the deployment would include members of Delta Force based at Fort Bragg, North Carolina, Major David Stockwell, speaking on behalf of the Pentagon in Somalia stated, he had "absolutely no knowledge of any Delta deployment. At this time it doesn't fit into our scenario."

Doorway to Hell

Pentagon officials remained silent about reports of a Delta Force involvement. "It is department policy never to discuss any of those special operations units," said LTC Joe Gradisher. However he mentioned "a task force made up of Rangers and other elements of U.S. Special Operations Command had deployed to Mogadishu."

At the very moment these statements were issued, Delta Force personnel had taken off from Fort Bragg and were on their way to Somalia.

By mounting daily RPG rocket, mortar and sniper attacks at UN military positions in Mogadishu, Aidid's militia had effectively taken back control of the neighborhoods, forcing the UN troops back to their bunkers and defensive positions. In addition, intelligence reports that Aidid had obtained shoulder mounted Soviet-built SA-7 surface-to-air missiles forced the UN to close Mogadishu's airport to civilian traffic on August 21.

On the same day that Aspin denied MG Montgomery's request for tanks to be sent to Somalia, UN Ambassador Madeline Albright stated publicly that the United States had "indications that a tactical alliance may be forming between Aidid's faction, terrorists based in the Sudan, and the government of Iran."

The Associated Press also reported a month later that the United States "strongly suspected" that Aidid's militia was obtaining both "training and weapons" from Sudan and Iran. The news service cited a "senior Clinton administration official" as stating that some of Somalia's weapons were coming from the Sudan and some from Kenya, without the government approval of Kenya.

Furthermore, the Associated Press reported that "intelligence sources" confirmed that Aidid's militia had received

111

large quantities of "remote-controlled mines complete with training on how to use them."[22]

In Washington, Congress was being increasingly dissatisfied with the Somalian operation. Congressman Bob Livingston (R-LA) stated, "The United States is on the verge of creating a force devoid of sustainable power and bereft of focus and direction. Clinton has turned on its head the old Teddy Roosevelt maxim to 'speak softly and carry a big stick,' instead he speaks interminably while brandishing a toothpick."

Senator Bob Dole complained in an August 31st letter to President Clinton that the United States seemed to be getting involved in too many areas where it lacked an immediate interest. He suggested that the U.S. should pull out of Somalia and stay out of Bosnia. He expressed his concern that the country could get into a long-term commitment involving substantial ground forces and money.

Representative Floyd Spence of South Carolina, the ranking minority member on the House Armed Services Committee, complained that defense department cuts were coming at a time when global commitments were increasing. An aide to Spence said the Congressman was concerned about "what degree the country can afford the force envisioned by Aspin, given Clinton's plan to cut at least $127 billion from the defense budget over the next five years."

The Republicans weren't the only ones worried about Somalia or the effects the expense of Somalia had on the budget. Democrats who were watching the polls were beginning to get nervous in view of the upcoming elections. The chairmen of the House and Senate Armed Services committees, Representative Ronald V. Dellums (D-CA) and Senator Sam Nunn (D-GA) expressed their open concerns about the Somalia deployments, especially about the change in mission from famine relief to law enforcement.

Within this military and political environment, McKnight's Rangers were ordered into Aidid-held territory in Mogadishu, without artillery, Spectre gunship, or tank support.

Late in the afternoon of Sunday, Oct. 3rd, 1993, attack helicopters dropped about 120 American soldiers, comprised of Delta Force and Rangers, into a busy neighborhood in the heart of Mogadishu. Their mission was to abduct several top lieutenants of Mohamed Farrah Aidid and return to base. It was a mission expected to last about forty five minutes.

But the planners underestimated the Somali firepower and will to fight. Instead of a surgical in-and-out operation, they took withering fire and two of their high-tech UH-60 Blackhawk attack helicopters were shot down. At one crash site one of the Blackhawk pilots had been killed in the crash and his body was still trapped in the wreckage. The Rangers were completely surrounded by a large group of armed Somalis intent on killing every American they could find.

For hours the men of Task Force Ranger were pinned down in the city streets fighting for their lives, and it was growing dark.

At the Mogadishu airfield, Lieutenant Colonel David, commander of Task Force 2-14, received the order to secure TF Ranger's exfiltration route. At 3:45 p.m., David moved out with one company via a ground convoy in an attempt to penetrate the city streets all the way to the crash site. But the Somalis had anticipated a relief column and had set up ambushes along the route. After traveling only one kilometer from the airfield, the convoy ran into a coordinated ambush that destroyed two Humvees and killed three soldiers, wounding four others. At this time contact was lost between the ground units that were attempting to maneuver out of the kill zones and proceed toward the embattled Rangers.

Still trying to move toward the crash site battle, David's units ran into several more ambushes that were placed along the route. David was forced to abort the mission and return to the airfield.

After consolidating his forces, LTC David received the word that the battle situation at the crash site was deteriorating and that a second Blackhawk had been shot down. By this time the ninety Rangers at the crash site were running dangerously low on ammunition and were receiving intense indirect and direct fire, the Ranger Ground Reaction Force had made four unsuccessful attempts to reach the crash site, and the Rangers had lost communication with a sniper team that had been inserted to cover the second crash site. David knew that if something wasn't done quickly, the Rangers would be overwhelmed after dark.

At 7:45 p.m., LTC David took command of a make-shift task force consisting of two Malaysian mechanized companies (drivers and gunners, but no infantry), a platoon from TF Ranger, two of his own rifle companies, and a Pakistani tank platoon that literally had to be prodded into action at gunpoint. He was to be supported by helicopter elements of TF 2-25 Special Ops Aviation detachment.

David's ad hoc relief group moved out at 11:00 p.m., and drove east around the port of Mogadishu, then north to National street. But as soon as the column turned west on National, the Somalis initiated another ambush. This time the guerrillas had anti-tank rockets and heavy machine guns emplaced.

As streams of automatic weapons fire laced into the convoy, David's subordinate leaders ordered return fire and forged ahead, knowing that to stop in a kill zone meant certain death. They eventually managed to break out of the ambush zone and rally at their release points. For the next three hours, Alpha Company of the 14th Infantry fought its way toward the embattle Rangers at the first crash site, and finally linked up with them in the early morning hours of the next day.

LTC David secured the site and made plans to recover the dead pilot's trapped body and all other casualties for evacuation, and push the Somalis back until the task force could reach the second crash site and see if anyone was left alive or there was anything to recover.

Charlie Company, 2/14 Infantry, under the command of Captain Michael Whetstone, pressed on and soon came under heavy small arms fire and rocket attacks from RPGs. Still, Whetstone's company fought on and managed to reach the second crash site. He reported back to David that there was nothing to recover and was ordered to link up with 2nd Platoon of A Company which by then was in close proximity, and to get back and make sure they didn't leave anyone behind.

When Whetstone found the 2nd platoon, which had been separated during the first ambush and had driven on in Malaysian APCs, he discovered that they had lost two APCs to rocket fire, and that there were "numerous Malaysian and American dead and wounded." He then found that the Malaysian battalion commander had ordered the Malaysians to leave the dead and wounded to preclude taking more casualties. CPT Whetstone radioed LTC David and informed him of the Malaysian orders. David replied "Stay the course. We will fight here as long as it takes. We will not leave any of our soldiers on the battlefield."

David's task force fought for four more hours, time enough to recover all the Rangers, wounded and dead. When they emerged the following morning, 18 Americans and one Malaysian were dead and 86 were wounded (57 Rangers and 29 TF David soldiers). And there was one MIA, helicopter pilot CWO Michael Durant, who had been dragged off by the Somalis, beaten severely, and was being held captive somewhere in the city. Several days would go by before he would be released.

The Somalis fared much worse. Estimates of Somali dead reached nearly 500, with more than a thousand estimated as wounded, many of which were women and children. This was hardly what U.S. leaders envisioned when Americans landed in Somalia in December 1992 to help avert starvation.

The disaster of the Ranger raid shocked the United States and had the same effect the Tet offensive had in 1968 during the Vietnam War. Americans began openly questioning, "What the Hell are we doing in Somalia? Why are we there? Why are American boys being killed by the people we're trying to help?." The problem was that these were legitimate questions that should have been asked by the White House, Congress and the Pentagon long before. Compounding the situation was the sudden realization that good intentions don't make good policy, and humanitarian operations can be euphemisms for war.

When Army Specialist Fourth Class Glenn Follett of Watertown, New York returned home from his tour in Somalia as a helicopter crewman, he summed up the perspectives of the others who were there, as well as those of his countrymen who suspected Somalia was a flawed policy in the first place and were now convinced the U.S. had drifted into a mini-war through the inattention of the White House. He said, "In the first two weeks I was in Somalia, I saw more combat than during six months in Saudi (Arabia). As soon as we stepped off the plane (in Somalia) we were getting shot at."

Now, with a political disaster on his hands and with front-page and television pictures of the beaten and bloody face of Chief Warrant Officer Michael Durant staring at him wherever he went,[23] President Clinton demanded of Aspin, "How did this happen?" President Clinton had finally learned that there is just so much you can delegate. On the other hand, Lyndon Johnson had learned that micro-managing was just as fatal.

Apparently no civilian in the administration had ever read Count Carl Von Clausewitz' treatise *On War*, published in the eighteenth century. Von Clausewitz warned almost two centuries ago that policy should "not extend its influence to operational details. Political considerations do not determine the posting of guards or the employment of patrols."[24]

What was worse was that Clinton had delegated the military to a Secretary of Defense whose introduction to the armed forces was to serve as a member of Robert McNamara's "whiz kid" team that attempted to micro-manage the Vietnam War from the Pentagon. Top military leaders who had graduated from the U.S. Army War College and other senior service schools were steeped in the principles of war as advocated by Von Clausewitz. However, civilians were running the Somalia operation and limiting the military on what they needed, what they could deploy, how they could utilize their weapons systems and under what conditions they could be used.

The civilian leadership in the Clinton administration quickly attempted to insulate themselves from any charge of malfeasance in case anything went wrong by standing on definition. If it was not "combat," so the reasoning went, military principles didn't apply. (Men like the 43d Engineer Battalion's Command Sergeant Major Lawrence Maxwell [who had served in Vietnam: 1968-69] could well have concluded that history was repeating itself and for the same reasons.) This time however, such rationale didn't hold up in the face of body bags being delivered back to the states, so the civilian officials began to scurry for cover and look for scapegoats.

By early Tuesday afternoon, October 5, National Security Advisor Anthony Lake had prepared a ten-page options paper for the President who was flying back to Washington aboard Air Force One. At 6:30 P.M. EST, Clinton met with his top advisors who hammered out a number of options in his presence. By the time the group broke up several hours later, they had agreed that the best strategy would be to reinforce the American troops in Somalia, shift from a "get Aidid" policy to a more political approach, and set a hard deadline for U.S. withdrawal.

The group reconvened over coffee at 8:45 P.M. Wednesday morning, supplemented by the attendance of Robert Oakley. By then, General Joseph P. Hoar, CENTCOM commander had forwarded a March 31, 1994 proposed withdrawal date. The date was arbitrary, but it provided time to restabilize the situation and negotiate a political settlement among clan elders and militia leaders without committing the U.S. to a dragged-out effort. When word arrived that an American unit had received mortar fire and another American soldier had been killed, Clinton overrode his Defense Secretary's decision and finally decided to send American armor to Somalia. Public opinion polls showed 89 percent of the American people wanted U.S. troops brought home as soon as possible; more important from the perspective of both the President and Congress, was Clinton's approval rating plummeting to 37 percent in the public opinion polls.

Republican Congressional leaders met with the President and questioned him vigorously about the continued wisdom of maintaining an American presence in Somalia. In separate meetings, Democrat Congressional leaders warned Clinton that

118

When American troops first arrived in Somalia, they were initially quartered in a tent city outside Mogadishu International Airport. (*All photos CPT Brian Wheeler*)

Eventually, they moved into more permanent facilities on the outskirts of the city.

Even though the entire country stank of death, and bodies were left to be consumed by wild animals and to rot in the sun ...

... Americans could still find some ways to bring laughter and joy to Somalian children, most of whom lived in misery and starvation.

Prominent buildings in downtown Mogadishu. Every building showed signs of previous heavy fighting. All windows were shot out and the masonry displayed the pockmarks of gunfire.

The presence of a fledgling oil industry was evident. U.S. engineers discovered an oil pipeline leading to the coast from a brand-new refinery that had been built just prior to the revolution. The oil tanker in the distance was partially sunk by gunfire during the revolution and the ensuing civil war.

The sea off Somalia is blue, cool and inviting. Unfortunately, it is also thick with sharks, which were attracted by the large number of human bodies that had been thrown into the water by warlords.

The Somalian people who were not affiliated with a warlord were barely surviving. They had no food, water or medical aid. Somalian men would fight to the death over an empty water bottle that had been discarded by a soldier.

Hospital support was non-existent and what medical aid that was available was provided in the open.

Transportation was so limited that almost all civilian vehicles were overloaded.

American, Canadian, Belgian and Italian troops discovered Soviet equipment scattered around the country from the coast to the Ethiopian border.

The "Big Bang" – the explosion that cleared the munitions from the abandoned Soviet surface-to-air missile (SAM) base. Photographed here from two miles away, the explosion ignited so many buried Soviet munitions that it shattered what few windows still remained in the city.

Australians and Americans were also sent to defend outback settlements such as Baidoa, Bardera, Washid and Kismayu, which were scattered across all of south central Somalia. Living in tent cities, they were subjected to mortar attacks, sniping and ambushes on a daily basis.

Operation Continue Hope picked up as Operation Restore Hope ended. Within days of the return of the 43rd Engineer Battalion to Fort Benning, Georgia, it was turned around and sent back to Somalia. The Engineers were then ordered to build "Victory Base" on the site of an old Soviet-built SAM base. To clear it, they blew up the old base and built a new one for an incoming tank battalion. After sending millions on the base, the U.S. withdrew from Somalia and "Victory Base" became the property of the warlord Mohammed Aidid.

Somalia had the potential for undercutting their continued control of Congress.

Ironically, Clinton was reduced to the same logic and arguments (which he rejected as an antiwar student protester) that President Lyndon Johnson used during the Vietnam War years. Clinton maintained that "the credibility of American power was at stake." He told the Congressmen that "the U.S. cannot just cut and run." That evening at 1700 hours, EST, Clinton announced to the nation that he was ordering to Somalia 1,700 more troops, 104 tanks, supporting Bradley Fighting Vehicles, and four Cobra attack helicopters."

Lyndon Johnson would have been pleased.

Chapter Seven

The Manipulation of Amateurs

It was now painfully obvious that the African warlord, Mohammed Farah Aidid, was far more experienced at manipulating the situation than was Clinton or his advisors. Not only had he served as the former commanding general of the Somalian Army and an ambassador from Somalia, but he was widely credited with having led the revolution against Siad Barre and was the clan leader of the Hawiye tribe, the largest in Somalia. Using his instincts and experience, Aidid maintained the initiative he had gained and called upon his supporters and all clans in Somalia for a cease fire. Speaking over a Mogadishu radio station he controlled, Aidid offered a truce to the United Nations and stated that Somali gunmen would not attack UN or U.S. troops unless they were attacked. This move gave Aidid the moral high ground and diplomatic and political initiative.

Doorway to Hell

Clinton finally realized that Aidid was more than merely the head of some equivalent Los Angeles street gang. He signaled Aidid that he was prepared to ignore the UN Security Council's resolution and include him in talks for a peaceful settlement.

Additionally, Clinton gave Oakley the authority to bypass the United Nations and negotiate directly with Presidents Meles Zenewi of Ethiopia, Issaias Afeworke of Eritrea, and other African leaders in order to achieve a peace in Somalia. Meanwhile, Clinton also indicated that the administration would do whatever it could to protect American troops and bring home those held "prisoner." The U.S. would also promote stability in Somalia for the six months it would remain there, but American troops would withdraw no later than March 31, 1994. Other than that, as long as Aidid's forces didn't attack U.S. troops, Clinton didn't much care what the Mogadishu warlord did.

With over two thousand troops and accompanying equipment being sent to Mogadishu, an operational and living area had to be prepared. Most of the available buildings were already occupied, so a base camp had to be built. The 43rd had been there before and was one of only three heavy construction battalions in the U.S. Army. It could build buildings, other hard structures and roads. Besides that, the Pentagon reasoned, the battalion was already familiar with the operation in Somalia. The alert arrived on October 8th, the first day of the Columbus Day weekend.

Some personnel in the 43rd who had been on extended high alert duty were given a three-day pass and had bailed out of Fort Benning for the long weekend. Most of the rest were at home with their families trying to recuperate from the horror they saw in Somalia. The Duty Officer and Duty NCO were left with little more than a lengthy sign out roster. One of those who had taken advantage of the long weekend was the battalion's signal officer, 1LT Brian Wheeler. Wheeler had flown home to Tulsa, Oklahoma, on Thursday evening. At 1715 hours, Friday, Wheeler was on the phone to Michael Veronis, a close friend since high school. Veronis asked Wheeler, a 1990 West Point graduate, if he would have to return to Somalia. The twenty-five-year-old lieutenant replied, "No way, we've performed our mission and besides that, the Battalion is due permanently deactivate next summer due to defense budget cutbacks, so I'm back in the States until then." Then the "call waiting" feature on his parents phone beeped. Wheeler tapped the switchhook and was told by the 43rd Engineer Battalion S-1 that they had been alerted and it looked as if "everybody" would be going back. Furthermore, his leave had just been canceled and he had to return to Fort Benning at once. He returned to his original call and said: "Mike, you aren't going to believe this!"

At Fort Benning, the 43rd's staff went quickly to work preparing the Battalion's Alfa Company and the Battalion's Advance Party for immediate deployment. To complicate the operation, the battalion had already turned in much of their equipment which had to be reacquired from Army channels. In short order the requirement to deploy to Somalia increased to the entire Battalion minus a rear detachment. Within the next few hours, change after change came down the command chain. Finally, LTC Davis and his staff decided to prepare for the worst case scenario, deployment of the entire Battalion at once. By the end of the weekend, that assumption proved closer to fact. Immediate packing and loading based on their recent experience put the Battalion's equipment on rail cars in record time. It was shipped to the port at Savannah to be loaded aboard the Bellatrix, the same ship that took their equipment to Somalia on the first deployment.

Doorway to Hell

Since construction material was not available in Somalia, the army component of Central Command (ARCENT) contracted with Brown & Root, Inc., to ship $1.7 million of construction material in sixty Milvans to Mogadishu. The Battalion purchased seven additional Milvans in which to build latrines and showers to meet immediate task force needs.

Nine days later, Captain Bernadine Thomson's Alpha Company's advance party boarded a C5A and flew to Mogadishu. The Battalion's advance party and the remainder of Alpha Company departed three days later on a commercial charter and landed at Cairo, Egypt. They transferred to a KC-10 in Cairo because commercial jets could not land in Mogadishu due to the increased threat. On Sunday, October 10th, the battalion's Advance Party landed at Mogadishu Airport Somalia to coordinate the arrival of the main body of the Battalion. As they stepped off the plane, they walked into a found themselves surrounded by firefights and mortar explosions. The city had deteriorated into absolute chaos. As they ran for the vehicles, Somalian fire whizzed over their heads.

At the same time the newly-arrived engineers stepped on Somalian soil for the second time, Secretary of State Warren Christopher appeared on NBC television's "Meet The Press" and admitted: "The effort to apprehend Aidid after his forces attacked Pakistani troops in June was a sound and natural response. I think it did get out of balance with too much focus on the military and not enough on the political side of the problem. I think we're all responsible for that, right up to and including the President."

In an administration that was focused on what Christopher described as the "big issues," the potential for serious harm to U.S. servicemen deployed in the strife-torn African nation never attracted the scrutiny of top decision makers, he said. Instead,

123

key issues of U.S. policy toward Somalia (including the ill-fated attempt to capture Somali warlord Mohammed Farah Aidid that U.S. officials then blamed for the retaliation slaying of the servicemen) were considered and decided by an interagency committee composed of lower ranking officials known as the "deputies committee." The committee, chaired by deputy White House National Security Advisor Samuel R. "Sandy" Berger, became the initial scapegoat. The chairman and members were blamed for not bringing the potential for trouble to the attention of more senior appointees.

On Wednesday, October 13, during a speech to the Washington Research Group, former Secretary of State James Baker said in an obvious allusion to President Clinton's promise to focus on domestic priorities: "It is fantasy to believe that foreign policy can be relegated to the back burner, or that Presidential responsibility can be delegated. The disaster in Mogadishu has prompted a reassessment on U.S. policy, or the lack of it."

Then on the following Friday, October 15th, during an interview with the Washington Post, Clinton admitted "I don't think we fully appreciated until several weeks ago just how much the management of the Somalian effort had been abandoned when we turned over the mission to the U.N. In the last month or so, we've been very busy dealing with Russia and the Middle East. Our attempts to keep that on track and go forward, both of which, in terms of our immediate national interest, are far more significant than our operations in Somalia."

On Tuesday, October 16, during a White House news conference, weeks after the U.S. Senate endorsed the March 31st deadline for the withdrawal of all American forces, Clinton desperately attempted to divert growing criticism of his handling of the Somalian situation. He accused former President Bush of "being naive." He also charged the United Nations with assigning American troops "the police function" of finding those responsible for the killing of twenty-four Pakistani soldiers. Then he said, "When Americans are imperiled, ultimately the president has to bear that responsibility. We erred in not realizing that the United Nations was changing the mission from a humanitarian one to a military and political one.

It may have been naive for anyone to seriously assert in the beginning that you could go into a situation as politically and militarily charged as that one, turn around and leave and expect everything to be hunky dory."

Both the President and the Secretary of State would have been better advised not to have pursued that line of thought in public. Former President George Bush still resented Clinton for hammering him during the Presidential campaign for not sending any troops into Somalia. After months of a partisan truce by the Republicans regarding Somalia, which was led by Senator Dole, the admission by Christopher followed by the partisan attack on Bush was more than the GOP could tolerate. The Republicans "smelled blood," and in the long tradition of Washington politics, they exercised the same option the Democrats used against Republican Presidents in office. They "ate the wounded."

Congressman James M. Inhofe (R-OK)[25], was one of the leaders of the Republican opposition. A member of the House Armed Services Committee, he called for the immediate resignation of Secretary of Defense Les Aspin, saying, "I am outraged that Secretary Aspin denied requests by the former Chairman of the Joint Chiefs of Staff, General Colin Powell, to send heavy armor to protect U.S. troops in Somalia. As the former Chairman of the House Armed Services Committee, I expected more from Secretary Aspin. However, it now appears that he is right at home in the administration which has already demonstrated a poor understanding of military leadership."

Dole, a disabled veteran who, ironically, was wounded in Italy during WWII while serving with the 10th Mountain Division, declared: "We have gotten ourselves in a situation of trying to capture an individual in the middle of an urban area he controls."

Clinton and his advisors were accused of messing up the operation that the Bush administration had handed over in "sound condition." In a stinging indictment, former President Bush blasted Clinton for "naively believing that a President could delegate foreign policy to subordinates while he focused on domestic affairs."

Speaking in San Antonio on Sunday, October 17, former President George Bush said, "If you're going to put somebody else's son or daughter into harm's way, into battle, you've got to know the answers to three questions. Those questions are, what is the mission, how is it going to get done, and how are they going to get out of there?" He continued with "When I sent American troops into Somalia last December, the mission was to save lives. People were starving, and American troops went in there, opened supply lines and they took food in. They weren't fighting, and when the Somali people were fed, the operation would be turned over to the UN, which is how we would get our troops home."

On October 18, during an interview with CNN, former Defense Secretary Dick Cheney said "When we originally went in to feed the Somalians, the United Nations pushed hard for us to broaden the mission, to define it as `nation-building', to say that we were going to disarm all of the warlords in Somalia. We refused to do that. What has happened since of course, is they (the Clinton administration) have gotten into difficulty because they didn't adhere to that very rigorous definition of what the mission is." He added that the "Clinton team seemed to be lacking in intellectual rigor and tight command and control."

What prompted the Bush team to speak out, said William Kristol, Chief of Staff to former Vice President Dan Quayle, was that the former President and his colleagues feared that with the situation deteriorating, it was essential to defend the idea of a tough-minded internationalism before the public debate degenerated into "McGovernite" quasi-isolationism on one side, and "Patrick Buchanon" isolationism on the other.

The political attack clearly wounded Clinton in the public eye and placed him and his administration on the defensive. Stung from the political broadsides, Clinton dispatched Oakley to try to bring together rival clan leaders. When word reached Aidid, he announced that he would "accept" a nonexistent cease fire offer from the United States. Clinton and Christopher also sent pleas to African leaders to join in promoting a peaceful settlement. In addition, the White House asked thirty other nations to commit or increase their military forces to replace the withdrawing Americans.

The departure date of March 31 announced by Clinton tended to calm the revolt that had been brewing in Congress and ironically led by Senator Harry Byrd (D-WV), Chairman of the Senate's Appropriations Committee. Whatever doubts they might have retained, however, the majority of lawmakers generally welcomed a firm deadline for withdrawal. It also represented a sort of declaration of independence from the United Nations and Boutros Ghali.

The new U.S. troops being sent to Somalia would be under American command, not that of the United Nations, and Oakley would operate as an American, not a UN negotiator or representative. Republicans had long suspected Boutros-Ghali of having delusions of grandeur. They delighted in quoting him as once having said U.S. troops would be withdrawn from Somalia "when I say they can come out." Bob Dole exulted that events had finally forced Clinton into a posture that meant that the U.S. would be doing, "what we were going to do, not [what] Boutros-Ghali [wanted]."

Besides demonstrating the skills of a clan leader, professional soldier and seasoned politician, Mohammed Farah Aidid also proved to be a skilled diplomat and propagandist. According to a confidential United Nations document, a month before his militia killed eighteen U.S. Rangers on October 4 he offered to cease hostilities and begin a "mutual dialogue" with the UN. The peace overture was rejected by the senior UN representative in Somalia, retired U.S. Admiral Jonathan T. Howe, according to John Drysdale, who resigned in September as Howe's political advisor.

Drysdale noted that it was accompanied by a demand that the United Nations cease offensive actions which was reasonable if negotiations were to begin in earnest, but a step that the United Nations was not then willing to take because Boutros Boutros-Ghali still wanted Mohammed Aidid in chains. In the back-channel discussions with Aidid, middle-level UN officials worked feverishly, at times without their superiors' knowledge, to hammer out a peace agreement even as the Rangers were crossing Mogadishu's skies on their way to the Olympic Hotel.

Although the process made considerable headway, according to Drysdale and documents provided by him, Howe passed up what Drysdale described as several chances to make peace with Aidid and instead chose a more aggressive course. Drysdale called the UN failure to take Aidid up on his peace offer as "absolutely scandalous." With that revelation, Boutros-Ghali lost more ground, for it was now obvious that he had passed up an opportunity for peace because of his personal animosity for Aidid.

Clinton and his advisors finally began to realize that the man who was pulling the strings of the whole situation was in Mogadishu, and it wasn't Admiral Howe. The President immediately ordered all American forces in Somalia to halt offensive operations against warlord Mohammed Farah Aidid while U.S. diplomats attempted to find a political solution to the conflict. Furious, Boutros-Ghali directed his spokesmen to continue to insist that Aidid remain subject to arrest by UN forces. American military commanders, however, were bound by the President's orders and not the United Nations, which infuriated Ghali, and stood down all operations which Aidid's militia could interpret as offensive.

Aidid had been a leader in the Somalian civil war. He kept a book on Chinese revolutionary tactics on the nightstand in the bedroom of his Mogadishu command compound, and, unlike the American president, was was also a student of military history. He told his staff about the lessons of the Tet offensive during the Vietnam War.

On October 14th, Aidid released Chief Warrant Officer Michael Durant, the Blackhawk helicopter pilot who was shot down during the raid on the Olympic Hotel, along with a Nigerian soldier seized by Aidid's militia on September 5th. Aidid announced that the release carried no conditions, but it was evident that he was hoping to improve his relations with the United States as the American mission shifted to promoting a political settlement.

On the same day Aidid held his press conference, Clinton held one of his own. He announced: "The United States being a police officer in Somalia was turned into the waging of conflict and a highly personalized battle. This had undermined the peace process and we intend to correct that within a few days."

This was intentionally meant to be an ill-concealed reference to the personal conflict between Boutros Ghali and Aidid. Additional comments made it clear that Clinton blamed the United Nations and specifically Secretary General Boutros Boutros Ghali for letting the situation get off track. Despite the fact that there was plenty of blame to go around, Clinton was trying desperately to avoid being personally targeted. Aspin meanwhile caught the brunt of the attacks.

Representatives Bill Archer and Sam Johnson of Texas circulated a letter through the House of Representatives encouraging Clinton to fire Aspin. At an October 28 press conference in Washington, Archer declared that Aspin was "guilty of inexcusable negligence in a Somalia policy that put political motivations above the safety of American troops. His integrity has suffered to the point where he can no longer be entrusted with the grave responsibility of this important post." Johnson, a retired Air Force fighter pilot who had spent seven years as a POW in North Vietnam blasted Clinton and Aspin for their refusal to refer to Chief Warrant Officer Michael Durant as a "prisoner of war" while he was being held by Aidid. By insisting that Durant was a mere 'detainee' for their own political reasons, the administration also deprived Durant of a U.S. Army POW medal, POW pay, and other benefits. As would become evident even later, this would be reflective of the Clinton administration's attitude and policies regarding the treatment of all of the U.S. veterans of Somalia.

In the face of growing criticism, the undeniable fact remained that the President and his staff had helped to draft and implement the UN strategy through the U.S. ambassador to the UN. Thus, the policy change Clinton announced, repudiated his own original policy.

Chapter Eight

The 43d Arrives...Again.

When the 43rd's Engineers deplaned from the KC-10 at Mogadishu International Airport, they achieved the distinction of being the only battalion to go to Somalia twice. Immediately, LTC Davis was informed that his Battalion would be attached to the "Falcon" Brigade, 10th Mountain Division, Joint Task Force, Somalia, and would provide direct support to Task Force 1/64 Armor.

Those who had returned to Somalia a second time were not thrilled by the prospect. Mogadishu was far different than the "outback." In fact it reminded them of Beirut, Lebanon after years of strife. It was so dangerous that any traveling, even on the periphery, had to be done with a minimum three-vehicle convoy that was heavily armed with crew-served weapons.
Upon arriving, the engineers were under sniper, mortar and automatic weapons fire until they reached a secure area.

Weapons were pouring into Somalia from other countries principally from Ethiopia. Mogadishu's open-air gun market featured everything from M-16 rifles to AK-47's. Ex-soldiers from the Ethiopian army, which disintegrated when that country's previous government collapsed in 1991, shipped arms into Somalia across the ill-defined desert border. Somalis in neighboring Kenya arranged other weapons shipments to their clansmen, with drug traffickers among the intermediaries. The arms were being brought into the country not only surreptitiously but also in huge shipments. One freighter was intercepted in the Indian Ocean, loaded to the gunwales with Somalia-bound arms from Serbia. A trading company in Cyprus arranged the shipment. When they did receive shipments however, the Somalian warlords quickly grasped the necessity to decentralize their arms caches, so throughout Mogadishu and other cities, small supplies of arms and ammunition were stored in individual houses.

Meanwhile, the 43rd Engineers operations section began its planning and arranged an aerial reconnaissance of the area to determine the best place for Victory Base. The impression that Mogadishu was one of the most dangerous places in the world wasn't the only opinion that the troops of the 43rd developed. As the 43d's Signal Officer wrote to his family on another makeshift postcard ripped off an MRE carton: "Well, here I am again. It seems as if I never left. Maybe I never did leave. Some things have changed while others stay the same. The politics and government red tape permeate the air around here, like the raunchy odor of my DCU's after 5 days of wear due to piss-poor laundry service. Of course last time we had no laundry service at all."

The difference between the first and second deployment was marked. When the battalion was assigned to Baidoa and the outback, they washed their uniforms on scrub boards, burned their latrines with fuel oil and sweltered in tents and Vietnam-era seahuts During the second deployment where they were assigned to the Mogadishu region, they had field showers, periodic laundry service, and contract sanitation removal service.

This time, the 43d was located in the middle of the hotbed of clan opposition. The UN. Intelligence on Aidid's guerrilla army had been refined and it was obvious that the gunmen were willing to fight even when faced with overwhelming firepower. Ground tacticians reported that the clansmen practiced excellent fire and movement skills with six to eight man squads. When they attacked, they would swarm an area with individual squads, and although they possessed poor lateral coordination and a pronounced lack of marksmanship, they made up for it by spraying a target area with automatic fire and RPG rocket launchers.

Aidid had also installed a highly sophisticated early warning system that notified his field commanders whenever UN personnel moved vehicles, units or lifted off helicopters. He also trained his personnel to pre-position debris for quick obstacle emplacements and roadblocks for ambushes. Additionally, the Somalian guerrillas proved to be very adept at using Soviet-made 60mm and 82mm mortars. Like the Vietcong guerrillas in the Vietnam war, they would habitually fire several rounds at a target, quickly break down the mortar and depart, making it extremely difficult, if not impossible, to return fire or discover their positions.

The warlords also had a fondness for gadgets. They used command detonated devices against soft targets such as Humvees and other light vehicles. Then the occupants who survived would be machine gunned after the explosion.

Being fully aware of the restrictive UN Rules of Engagement imposed upon the allied forces, the warlords occasionally used females and adolescents to leave booby traps and explosive devices in areas where a man would come under suspicion.

Additionally, crowds of Somalians could be gathered quickly and agitated into demonstrations, so the warlord gunmen could use the confusion for cover, concealment and sniping. Since there were numerous three and four story buildings along high speed mobility corridors, all vehicles had to be protected by alert personnel watching the windows and roofs from which either small arms fire, grenades, RPGs, or molotov cocktails could be thrown ontoa convoy.

While on a mission, U.S. Army Sergeant Timothy Carter drove his open Humvee through the streets of Mogadishu with two gunners sitting on the back, eyeing the crowds. As the vehicle slowed, several Somalies rushed forward. While the two guards fought off the crowd, one armed Somali jumped into the passenger seat. Suddenly Carter felt a knife blade up against his neck. He turned slowly and saw a young Somali man holding the clan knife. Carter mentally counted to three and lifted his right elbow in a quick move, smashing it into the Somali's mouth. The blow knocked the attacker out of the Humvee. He survived the attack with only a few knife nicks on his neck. Earlier, that same week Carter was on another street on foot patrol when a rock smacked him in the neck. Carter saw the rock thrower and through an English-speaking Somali who was nearby, told the rockthrower to stop. The next rock struck Carter in the jaw. The Rules of Engagement prevented Carter from using his weapon and he couldn't pursue the assailant or run the risk of being swallowed up by the surrounding crowd, so he simply had to withdraw.

This was the environment in Mogadishu into which the 43d Engineers were landed.

Unlike its first tour in Somalia, this time the 43rd had a specific mission to "bed down" Task Force 1/64[26] while maximizing force protection and quality of life for the assigned soldiers. The 43rd Engineers identified an abandoned Soviet missile construction facility three kilometers north of Mogadishu as a possible base area.

The location was ideal, and LTC Davis was going to go all out with his engineers to build the best facility possible with what was at hand.

Scouting the location proved that it had good drainage, an existing road network, was easy to secure and defend, and it was out of the range of 60mm mortar rounds launched from the back alleys of the Aidid-controlled portion of the city. But, one problem existed. The site contained over eighty-four thousand pounds of warheads and rocket propellant from abandoned missiles requiring an additional 10,000 pounds of TNT to obliterate them. The destruction of the Soviet ordnance resulted in a huge explosion which mushroomed into the sky. The shock waves carried across the city and knocked people off their feet more than two miles away.

This time the 43rd wouldn't be going in-country, but instead would be devoting its entire time and resources to the building of a sixteen hundred man camp that was named "Victory Base" after the Victory Brigade of the 24th Infantry division to which the 1st Battalion, 64th Armor was assigned. It was around this battalion that the Task Force was structured.

LTC Davis, who realized upon his return to Somalia that he had become the in-country senior engineer officer, immediately followed the pattern of the initial deployment and conducted meetings to coordinate all engineer assets and operations. Under his command, the 43rd's Engineers quickly went to work after the demolition of the Soviet material.

Hundreds of tons of twisted metal and rubble left by the blast were removed. More than 3.7 million square feet was cleared, and 880,000 square feet of crushed coral was emplaced.

A berm, road, ammunition supply point, test fire pit, and fuel dump sites were built.

Following that phase, they constructed 162 various sized Vietnam-era designed seahuts from 30-year blueprints they still had in their files. These would house both personnel and equipment, all supplied with electricity and some even with portable air conditioners..

Additionally, they built twelve Milvan guard towers, a large, strongback chapel, laundry and bath facilities, bunkers, and a power grid installation. They added a twenty-five-meter small arms qualification range; detention facility; a small air-conditioned post exchange; decks, benches, and privacy screens for shower trailers; two hundred pieces of modular furniture; a fitness trail with seven exercise stations; and baseball and soccer fields complete with backstop, goalposts, bleachers, and even a line chalker. The base was completed five weeks after the area was cleared with the "Big Bang."

While they were performing these missions, elements of the Battalion also completed engineering projects at the JTF (Joint Task Force) headquarters, Checkpoint 31, so-called "Gotham City" at Sword Base at the Mogadishu Airport where they waterproofed the terminal roof and prepared the site for the proposed new JTF headquarters.

Another assignment was to reconnoiter possible base locations. Their reconnaissance led them to a former boat factory nicknamed by former occupiers "The Flybase." The complex of buildings, approximately twenty five kilometers south of Mogadishu on the coastline, still had hulls of fiberglass boats inside both of the two main warehouses. When the 43rd's Engineers arrived, they found the facility under control of the Indian Army. After explaining their purpose and negotiating their needs, they were escorted into the facility by the Indian soldiers. Inside one of the warehouses was a concrete blockhouse without windows and with only one rusty door as an access.

The concrete structure was covered with swarms of flies and emanated a sickly sweet odor. Although the local Somalis would crawl through raw sewage and empty portable toilets for one dollar per hour, none of them would go anywhere near the building and would not talk about it. When the S-3 of the 43rd, Major Mark Feierstein squeezed past the rusty and salt-air corroded metal door and entered utter darkness. He flicked on his flashlight and saw a mass of decaying and dismembered flesh and bones on the floor and hanging from the walls. Quickly overcome by the odor of what was obviously death, fecal matter, decaying flesh and assaulted by swarming flies, he bailed out of the small concrete building before he threw up. Other members of the Battalion who entered the building and witnessed the mass of flesh and bone left quickly as well. It reminded one officer of what it must have looked like to have liberated Dachau or Buchenwald in 1945.

Nobody was ever able to determine the origin of the "Flybase." The Somalis wouldn't talk about it and the Indian army contingent reported that it was there when they arrived. The media never mentioned it--which was no surprise since few members of the press ever ventured out of Mogadishu.

Members of the 43rd concluded that based on the contents and the reactions of the local Somalis, the "Flybase" had been a torture chamber for one of the warlords before the Indian Army arrived. For that matter, it might have served the same function for Siad Barre, prior to his overthrow. Barre's opponents would disappear with a regularity that matched those opponents of the warlords, and the "Flybase" could easily have been their last destination.

Barre was known to have maintained torture houses in Mogadishu and could easily have had similar locations near the capitol.

One of the favorite forms of torture was the "Somalian Split" practiced by the Somalian Security Police. The victim would be spreadeagled between four poles above a shallow pit filled with starving rats. The security police would then slice open the victim's torso from the xiphoid bone in the chest to the groin and peel back the skin and underlying muscle tissue. The intestines would fall from the body into the pit and the victim would die screaming. The victim however would live just long enough to see the rats begin to feed on what had emptied out of his own torso. A second prisoner who was being interrogated would be made to watch. It was reported that the process always produced the information the security police wanted. Other techniques of torture were equally brutal and bloody and there was ample evidence that they were practiced by the warlords as well.

In any event, the 43rd's reconnaissance concluded that the boat factory would not serve their needs so they left the factory and the "Flybase" in the hands of the Indian Army.

Besides the 43rd Engineers, other American reinforcements also poured into Somalia. By November 5 there were 7,600 U.S. troops on the ground in-country, chiefly assembled in the Mogadishu area and backed by an additional 3,700 Marines offshore and on an aircraft carrier. Two heavily-armed AC-130 specter gunships had arrived, together with 30 M1A1 tanks, 42 Bradley Fighting Vehicles, and a battery of 155mm howitzers. No longer would American forces be without dependable armor, air, or artillery support.

The Battalion was assisted in their construction projects by the Brown & Root Construction Company, Inc., based in

Doorway to Hell

Houston, Texas, which provided equipment and supplies. Brown & Root could afford to. It had become one of the largest government contractors in U.S. history. Despite the already existing Kennedy Space Center in Florida, the company was awarded a $90 million contract on a "cost plus" basis to build the NASA Space Center twenty-two miles from Houston on a desolate tract of desert land owned by a Texas oil company. At the time the contract was granted, Lyndon Johnson was head of the Space Council.

A federal investigation of Brown & Root for violation of the Federal Corrupt Practices Act was dropped in the early 1940's by order of President Franklin Roosevelt. The company had been charged with violating the five thousand dollar campaign donation limit to Lyndon Johnson by rebating subcontractors. Later during the Vietnam War, despite the existence of a deep-water port at Da Nang which could have been expanded economically, Johnson and his "military advisors" selected Camh Ranh Bay, a shallow inlet only 150 miles north of Saigon. The bay, which offered little protection to large cargo ships, was too shallow to permit close-in unloading. In spite of this condition, Johnson insisted that Cam Ranh Bay be developed. This meant millions of dollars in dredging costs alone, not mentioning runway and base construction. Brown & Root was awarded the contract even though the South Vietnamese wanted the work-- and at much less cost to the America taxpayer. During the Persian Gulf War, Brown & Root was also a prime contractor, providing equipment and materials in the buildup of U.S. forces in Saudi Arabia and Bahrain.

When the 43rd departed Mogadishu, it signed over to Brown & Root much of its rolling stock and equipment. The transfer was classified as "Government Furnished Equipment" which was needed by Brown & Root to haul fuel, food, and supplies and

139

perform additional construction projects. The contract also called for Brown & Root to return the equipment to Fort Polk, Louisiana, when they completed their work. There it would be overhauled, brought up to operating standards and reassigned throughout the army.

The 43rd wouldn't need the equipment again. Due to defense budget reductions, it was scheduled to be deactivated on July 15, 1994.

The 43rd wasn't the only command supported by Brown & Root. The Houston firm became the largest contractor in Somalia and the operation's logistical arm. UNOSOM requested $94 million from UN headquarters in New York to pay for the company's services through the spring of 1994.

Under the cost-plus contract, Brown & Root was paid a fee based on performance up to 9 percent of total costs. By early spring, 1994 Brown & Root received $4.5 million under the provisions of the contract. Contracts awarded to Somalians were minuscule in comparison, since few local companies had the resources to support the operation. UNOSOM hired more than eighteen hundred Somalis for tasks ranging from ditch digging to sewage disposal to translation services. Yet, the fact that the overwhelming majority of the operation's money went to companies from elsewhere in the world was widely known among the Somalis and represented still an additional source of aggravation directed at the United Nations.

Where the Somalis were aggravated, American combat troops were humiliated by their own command structure.

On December 2, on order of Robert Oakley, an American military transport picked up Mohammed Farah Aidid at Mogadishu's airport and flew him to a peace conference of Somalia's warring clans in Addis Ababa, Ethiopia. U.S. Army troops from the Falcon Brigade of the 10th Mountain Division were now ordered to be bodyguards for the Somalian warlord. The troops assigned to personal security duty for Aidid were from the same unit that had lost five of their buddies to Aidid's forces on October 3rd while attempting to relieve the besieged American Rangers during the battle of "No-Name Street".

The humiliation forced upon these troops, plus the idea that U.S. forces would transport the man who was principally responsible for the American losses, infuriated Americans. Veterans' groups such as the American Legion, Veterans of Foreign Wars, Military Order of World Wars, and Disabled American Veterans flooded the White House and Congress with protests on behalf of those still serving, since active soldiers do not have the option of participating in the political process.

The heat was felt in the White House almost immediately.

Clinton was trying to divert the nation's attention to his proposed health plan, but he was being constantly interrogated with questions by media and Congressmen about why the U.S. "humbled itself" and "humiliated its troops" by flying Aidid to Ethiopia. Clinton explained that he supported Robert Oakley's decision in order to expedite the peace process. However, this just infuriated veterans' groups even more.

Desperate for a way out, and trying to salvage his own political hide, Clinton signaled Aspin that it was time for a new Defense Secretary. On December 14, Defense Secretary Les Aspin "tendered" his resignation for "personal" reasons. Although the President "accepted it with regret," Aspin's mismanagement of the entire operation in Somalia was cited by his critics as the principle reason he had to go.

While Clinton was rolling Aspin's head to save his own, Victory Base was being completed and TF-1/64 from Fort Stewart, Georgia rolled in.

1LT Paul Terrell of C Company said, "Most of the shooting and everything seems to have stopped since the tanks and heavy forces started arriving, so I think we're doing the job just by being here." He added, "We're ready to go. The guys here are chomping at the bit. We've been here for three weeks now. We're just ready to do something."

Meanwhile, LTC Davis was acutely aware that his command represented a unique asset to the theater of operations. He focused the efforts and resources of his engineers on completing the mission of building "Victory Base" and performing some of the corollary assignments. He knew that if he did not get the Battalion out of the country as soon as they were through, somebody in JTF headquarters would realize that the 43rd was the only vertical construction battalion in-country and "mission creep" would occur. If that happened, there would be no telling how long the battalion would be kept there. Davis had to walk a fine line because he did not want to be perceived as a "complainer," but he also did not want his troops kept in-country after they had completed the precise mission for which they had returned to Somalia a second time to perform.

Routinely and quietly they stood down their operation, turned over their equipment to Brown & Root, packed and loaded their personal gear, and made preparations to return home. If everything went well, they would make it home before Christmas. Then, within days of their scheduled departure, it suddenly dawned on staff personnel at JTF headquarters that the 43rd was about to depart. Hurried staff recommendations were made to keep the Battalion in-country, but Major General Carl Ernst, Commander of the Joint Task Force, overruled his own staff and ordered Davis and his Battalion to depart for home.

While Washington D.C. was in turmoil in the wake of the resignation of Secretary of Defense Les Aspin, the 43rd

Doorway to Hell

Engineer Battalion loaded aboard a 747 at Mogadishu airport and flew to Cairo, Rome, Paris, and then to Atlanta, Georgia. The plane stayed on the ground at each location just long enough to refuel, so the soldiers were not allowed to deplane due to the threat of possible terrorist attacks. As Davis later commented: "The troops would have enjoyed getting off the plane and stretching their legs, but since they couldn't, they made the best they could out of the situation just as they had in Somalia."

The plane landed at Atlanta International Airport and the troops were transferred to commercial buses, which took them to their families awaiting them at Lawson Army Airfield. Ironically, on the way one of the buses broke down. After all they'd been through in Somalia, they couldn't help but see the humor in the breakdown of a modern commercial bus on an American highway. The soldiers immediately transferred to the remaining buses, causing considerable distraction to passing civilian drivers since the engineers were still fully equipped with their weapons, ammunition, and were dressed in all of their desert battle gear.

Shortly after the transfer, they arrived at Fort Benning and unloaded their buses on the tarmac at Lawson Army Airfield. Command Sergeant Major Maxwell organized the troops into a battalion formation in front of a familiar, rusting, WW II hangar as two soldiers slowly pushed open the doors and the sounds of cheers and the musical notes of *An American Soldier* filled the cold morning air.

The 43rd was home.

Again.

Chapter Nine

Operation Continue Hope - 1994

Twenty-four hours after the rest of the world celebrated the New Year, Somali gunmen raided the World Food Compound in Baidoa. One Somali was killed and a second one was wounded in the raid which stripped the compound of its stored rations. A UN official, who spoke only on condition his name not be used, stated that UN analysts believe the raid was part of a larger campaign by Muslim extremists against non-Muslim aid agencies. Another UN official from a European nation who understandably demanded anonymity, was more pointed in his analysis: "Most social systems are bell curved at the sophisticated and civilized end. Somalia bulges at the opposite end. These people are no more civilized than they were 2,000 years ago when they came out of the trees."

U.S. forces were no longer in Baidoa. In fact, except for a contingent of U.S. Marines aboard ships off coast as a strike force to protect one thousand American employees of the UN, all American servicemen would be out of the country by March 25th. However, it was a long road from January 1st for those left in that devastated country and it would be a rough three months.

By the beginning of the year, it had been determined that the photographs of Somalis dragging stripped and dead American Special Forces troops down "No-Name Street" showed Army Master Sergeant Gary Gordon, Lincoln, Maine, and Staff Sergeant Thomas J. Field, from Lisbon, Maine. The sight of the dishonoring of the American dead enraged the nation. When the National Executive Committee of the American Legion met in Indianapolis, the members unanimously passed several resolutions, two of which reflected the opinion of the majority of Americans. Resolution 15 "urged" the President and Congress not to put American forces under foreign command without specific Congressional approval. Resolution 33 called for the "immediate withdrawal of all American forces from Somalia." Following that, the head of the largest veterans' organization in the United States, National Commander Bruce Thiesson of the America Legion promptly blasted President Clinton: "The nature of the mission and role of U.S. troops is questionable. American troops have been placed under foreign command. In our view, that violates the U.S. Constitution unless Congress approves." He further added: "U.S. troops should be pulled out because they are not protected by the Geneva Convention if they are taken hostage or become political prisoners during peacekeeping or humanitarian missions."

The American Legion then initiated a campaign to enlist members throughout the country to pressure their state legislatures to pass memorializing resolutions which would be sent to their respective state Congressional delegations.

On January 9th U.S. forces became involved in another brutal shootout. At 3:20 P.M. Marine Corps Special Operations forces, assigned to the UN position known as K-7 located just east of the U.S. Embassy compound, engaged a Somali gunman carrying a Soviet-made RPK light machine gun.

An hour and thirty-five minutes later, U.S. troops heard gunfire from the southwest corner of the Benadir Hospital compound located east of the embassy. Shortly after the shooting, the body of a dead Somali woman who was eight months pregnant was delivered to the Marines' position at K-7. An angry Somali crowd accused the Marines of killing the woman and her unborn baby.

Based on the U.S Rules of Engagement the Marines were ruled to have been in compliance since the Somali gunman was armed with a machine gun. A subsequent review by the command of the Joint Operations Task Force to which the Marines were attached determined that the Americans were in compliance with UN ROE as well. Under UN ROE, the action by the Marines was ruled "justifiable" because the UN "allowed," but did not "require," UN troops to open fire on Somalis armed with machine guns or crew-served weapons.

"It's a judgment call," said Colonel Steven Rausch, director of the U.S. Joint Information Bureau in Mogadishu. "Unless they have a good shot they are not required to take it," he said, "they do not just blaze away."

However, the issue of the shooting erupted into an argument between U.S. officials and Pakistanis. Pakistani troops were also stationed at the K-7 intersection but did not open fire. The Marines at K-7 accused the Pakistanis of not firing for "fear of provoking the locals." The Pakistanis responded by implying that they were "doing their job with the utmost care, and the Americans take too many risks when they open fire." Shortly thereafter, the Marine contingent was withdrawn from K-7, leaving the post entirely under control of the Pakistani contingent. This was fine with the Marines who manned that position. They never felt comfortable with an ally who was undependable when the chips were down, because it was obvious that the Pakistanis were drawing more pay from the UN than they could ever make as simple Pakistani soldiers, and they wanted to draw it out as long as possible. They didn't want to offend the Somalians and become the source of an international incident, to be ordered withdrawn and sent back to Pakistan to duty on the Indian border.

Meanwhile, controlled chaos replaced absolute anarchy in Mogadishu. Enterprising Somalis found ways to make some things work even without a formal structure. In fact, Somalia may conceivably be the only country in the world where a bureaucracy developed as an independent entity without a government to serve. Much of what is done in Mogadishu would be illegal if there were any laws to be broken or any lawmakers to write them.

The Somali immigration office was plundered following the revolution. Among the documents stolen were blank passports and passport stamps. The price for a Somali to get a passport on the Mogadishu black market was 70,000 Shillings ($20 U.S.), and 105,000 Shillings ($30 U.S.) for those shopping for diplomatic immunity.

Mogadishu became a classic case study for sociologists and economists. Markets bloomed without government regulation, while corruption thrived just as much in the absence of government officials. One of the key places also looted was the Somalian Central Bank which provided the country's money supply. Under normal conditions, currency printed by a government no longer in existence is worthless. However, in Mogadishu, an unwritten agreement developed that shillings would continue to be accepted, in spite of the fact that no agency existed to print new bills and no banks remained to distribute them.

In southern Mogadishu, controlled by Aidid, the exchange rate for old shilling notes is set by a few big dealers in the Bakahara Market. In northern Mogadishu, the stronghold of Ali Mahdi Mohammed, people use new shillings that had been ordered by Siad Barre's government but were looted before they could be distributed.

Faced by gunmen roving throughout the city, many Mogadishu neighborhoods set up security patrols or hired their own mercenaries to fight off looters. Camel dealers walked their herds as far as 280 miles to the Garasbaley Camel Market, a pungent, dusty lot in Ali Mahdi territory where three hundred camels might be exchanged in a day. The dealers and herders teamed up to pay guards and to corral rustlers who tried to fence stolen animals. To avoid trouble, and keep the camel supply flowing smoothly, Aidid's supporters had their own market. However, as in the neighborhoods, the danger remained that herds would be rustled by roving gunmen. The herders also complained that UN troops wouldn't let them keep enough guns to protect themselves or their animals when they are on the road toward Mogadishu.

Among priorities for the UN, the establishment, training, and equipping of a police force in Mogadishu were at the top of the list. With the help of American Army military police and training personnel from the German Army, the process began. However, with two warlords dividing the city, the UN negotiated co-chiefs of the police force.

Through arbitration with Mohammed Farah Aidid, one of his supporters was selected as a co-chief. Former Somali General Ahmed Jilao Addo was also appointed, and the new members of the Mogadishu police force were placed under his command.

Doorway to Hell

Unfortunately, Addo had been Siad Barre's Heinrich Himmler. He ran Barre's notorious political prison for years. It was known among Somalis as "Jilao's Hole." Those who entered seldom walked out, and the few who survived told tales of brutal torture and summary executions. Addo's new job as co-chief of the Mogadishu police force left many Somalis frightened, disappointed, and enraged at the UN. The Mogadishu police force had commanded a large measure of respect prior to the revolution despite Addo, but without the professionalism that used to be present Addo represented a distinct danger in the eyes of many Somalis. Armed by Egypt and the United States and trained by German police, the newly formed Mogadishu police force represented the promise of eventual stability. However, with Addo as co-chief, the credibility of the force was undercut overnight. Yet, the UN felt it had to achieve some progress, and with Aidid insisting on Addo it was left with very little option according to a UN spokesman.

On Friday, January 22, 1994, a top clan elder and thousands of his people marched back and forth across Mogadishu's treacherous cease-fire line for several hours, demanding an end to the ongoing violence. Accompanied by the elder, Imam Mohammed Imam Omar, and officials from Mogadishu's two warring clans, exuberant men, women, and children cheered "Today is a great day" and waved purple flowers. On Sunday, January 24, officials and supporters of Mohammed Farah Aidid met at a hotel in northern Mogadishu. They drew up a peace accord for their area of the capital and promised to "severely" punish anyone breaking it under harsh laws they would establish. Within days, Ali Mahdi and officials of Aidid's Somali National Alliance supported the reconciliation agreement signed by their clan elders.

149

Doorway to Hell

By the end of January, relief agencies beyond the borders of Mogadishu began to pull out their personnel. At Belet Huen, two hundred miles north of Mogadishu, fifty Somali gunmen shot their way into a World Food Program warehouse and looted 340 tons of food. Allegations were made by World Food Program officials that nearby Italian troops failed to respond to emergency calls for help. The World Food Program also announced that its personnel would be evacuated from Somalia due to a lack of security.

In the same city, Save The Children relief workers were faced with an attack on their warehouse and radioed the nearby Italian Army command headquarters. According to Save Our Children officials, they were "categorically denied" support by Italian troops. Italian officials denied the allegation and pointed out that their primary mission in Belet Huen was to protect 1,300 German soldiers who were in the city to transport material. In response to the failure of the Italians to provide security, the Save Our Children headquarters in Mogadishu ordered the evacuation of its staff from Belet Huen.

While the looting of the relief agencies went on at Belet Huen, Mohammed Farah Aidid dined in a luxury hotel suite in Nairobi, Kenya. From there he conducted informal negotiations with rivals and allies, periodically issuing proclamations of peace. Despite peaceful intentions and declarations, violence continued supplied by third-parties who wanted to have an influential role in whatever direction Somalia went. Competing for credit was Iran which was trying to sway Somalia into a fundamentalist role, private citizens in Saudi Arabia who are trying to keep Somalia out of the fundamentalist camp, and the Sudan and Ethiopia which were simply profiting on supplying arms, ammunition and training.

150

Doorway to Hell

On February 1, a five-vehicle convoy carrying twenty-two U.S. Marines guarding two American diplomats was enroute from the U.S. embassy compound to a meeting with officials of Mohammed Farah Aidid to discuss the continuing violence. The convoy was fired upon by Somali snipers. The Marines returned the fire and a brief battle erupted. Three Somali bullets struck the HUMVEEs in which the Marines and diplomats were riding, but none of the occupants were hit. After the battle, eight Somalis were dead and twenty-four were wounded. One of the dead was identified as a Somali tribal leader, Sabryie Alale Barise. Foreign correspondents in a nearby hotel heard several shots before the Marines reacted. Once the Marines returned the fire, the battle was joined by other armed Somalis in the vicinity, but the Marine convoy continued and eventually fought its way out of the area.

The commander of a Bangladeshi military force at a nearby intersection reported that he heard the gunfire but was "too far away" to render assistance. Later he reported "dozens of Somalis running through his area carrying the dead and wounded in wheelbarrows." The ambush occurred near the intersection commanded by 150 Bangladeshi troops who were mounted behind sandbagged bunkers on the tops of two adjoining buildings. The diplomatic meeting to discuss the continuing violence was canceled.

With the pending withdrawal of U.S. troops and the military power they represented, Somali guerrillas became more aggressive. Several days after the ambush, a hand grenade and a land mine exploded at the compound of a British Army mine-clearing company which was involved in a labor dispute with Somalis in northwest Somalia. At the same time, American soldiers killed an armed gunman near the new port area in Mogadishu.

151

Doorway to Hell

On February 8th the Deputy Commander of UN forces in Somalia, MG Thomas Montgomery, unceremoniously doffed his blue beret as he left his post. Leaving behind 4,500 U.S. troops who were also preparing to withdraw, he remained in command of all U.S. forces until the last contingent left on March 25.

Almost as a farewell salute while Montgomery was departing, a huge explosion blew a hole in the wall of the Mogadishu compound of World Vision, an international Christian charity. The blast prompted the organization to evacuate its staff. On the same day an Italian army convoy was ambushed in central Somalia killing Lieutenant Guilio Ruzzi, twenty-eight, and Private Franco Ratteni, twenty. Within hours of the ambush, an Italian civilian working for International Committee for the Development of Peoples was kidnaped. Somali gunmen also threw up roadblocks between the UN compound and the Mogadishu International Airport which had to be broken up at gunpoint by an allied rapid deployment force.

By the end of February, a new threat started to appear on the Somalian horizon. An epidemic of cholera began in the northern part of the country and finally spread to Mogadishu when scores of Somalis in the capital city began showing symptoms. More than 3,600 Somalis contracted cholera, and the pure volume of victims quickly overwhelmed the rudimentary health care system. In some areas of Somalia the infection rate increased by 900 percent in a single week, with most victims being children. Since cholera is spread through contaminated water, the seasonal rains that started in April prolonged the season of death.

The few UN workers who were able to reach wells without being ambushed chlorinated the water supply. UN information personnel asked Somali radio stations to broadcast appeals to the largely illiterate population regarding what measures to take to avoid cholera. The radio stations demanded sixty dollars for each public service announcement. When the Imams were asked to disseminate information at their Muslim mosques, they likewise demanded money. Clan leaders and editors of Mogadishu's crude newsletter-style newspapers also demanded payment. In a country where clan hatred and mistrust is so deeply rooted, not even a killer disease is a common enemy. In one hard-hit Mogadishu neighborhood, French aid workers could not set up a cholera clinic because neither sub-clan would agree to locate it in the territory of its rival.

As the withdrawal date for the last American troops approached, clan gunmen jacked tensions up another notch with increased attacks on the remaining American forces. On Wednesday, February 24th, Somali gunmen sprayed the Mogadishu Airport with machine gun fire but were driven off by U.S. troops inside the terminal area. Twenty-four hours later Marines killed a Somali who aimed an American M-16A1 rifle at their guardpost. (The American-made rifle had been previously issued to Somalians by the CIA to assist them during the Somalian-Ethiopian War.) This was the third Somali gunman killed at that guardpost in ninety minutes. Just an hour and a half before, two others had tried the same tactic with the same results.

On March 2nd, the Falcon Brigade of the U.S. Army's 10th Mountain Division, which had been supported by LTC Davis' 43rd Engineer Combat Battalion, said a final goodbye to Somalia. Five members of that brigade had gone home earlier in body bags. They had been killed in the fighting to relieve the embattled Rangers on "No-Name Street".

As the month of March passed, firing continued in downtown Mogadishu and began to creep closer to the airport. Somali factions were settling old debts with gunfire. Neither UN officials or remaining U.S. troops knew or cared who was involved or who won.

On Thursday, March 25, amid the din and dust of helicopters and armor, American troops ended their mission in Somalia and returned to their homes, ships, or bases. "Operation Quickdraw," the highly orchestrated withdrawal of the last Marines, began moments after a giant C-5A Galaxy cargo aircraft carrying about fifty men lifted off the runway of the Mogadishu Airport bound for Dover, Delaware.

The rear guard detachment lumbered into the surf a little over two hours later and boarded an amphibious assault vehicle. The rear guard was commanded by Marine Lieutenant David Wolcott, 24, of Newtown, Connecticut. He said to journalists on the beach, "I suggest you get out of here while you can." With that admonition, he battened down his hatch and headed his amphibious vehicle in the direction of a U.S. Navy transport vessel.

At the same time, the gates of Mogadishu's port were knocked to the ground, warehouses were looted, and weapons were seized in full view of Egyptian Army sentries--troops from Boutros Ghali's own country. All UN and civilian relief agencies evacuated their personnel from outlying cities and regions. Looters descended upon the airport even before American Marines lifted off in their helicopters. The seaport was overrun as Somalis breezed past Egyptian sentries with counterfeit passes, weapons, and booty.

Ed Johns, a lanky Texan appointed by the United Nations to run the port, said that he needed to hire Somali guards to provide internal security. He reported that looters were so prevalent that they managed to carry items as large as washing machines and generators past Egyptian military guards. One night sixty tires went past the sentries, apparently unnoticed. During another night fifteen high pressure pumps were stolen.

The UN force was made more inefficient by cultural and language barriers. Pakistani troops refused to escort some food convoys on Fridays, the Muslim sabbath. Somalis, stressing brotherhood with the Egyptians, routinely talked their way past Egyptian sentries.

On April 1, gunmen abducted an American Red Cross worker and killed his Somali guard in a shootout near the UN headquarters in southern Mogadishu. As the level of violence accelerated, the UN responded with more restrictive Rules of Engagement. No longer were UN troops permitted to fire on "technicals," but were ordered to use "minimum force" under all situations. Previously, "technicals" were engaged on sight. This automatically created a pronounced reluctance on the part of UN troops to exercise any authority whatsoever. The result was utter chaos despite protestations that the UN was "making progress" and that the "overall security system had improved" after the Americans left.

From December 3, 1992 through March 25, 1994, Operation Restore Hope had become Operation Continue Hope. Nobody in Washington wanted to go on record as pointing out that it had evolved into "Operation Abandon Hope."

On April 6, 1994, Mohammed Farah Aidid appeared before seven hundred delegates of the Pan-African Conference in Kampala, Uganda and incredibly demanded that the United Nations pay reparations for the "13,000 deaths of Somalian citizens caused by the UN peacekeeping force that was deployed there."

At the same time, Michael Harper, Director of the United Nations Association-United Kingdom said on his return from a UNICEF-funded mission to Somalia: "The UN humanitarian effort had been largely successful, but the military operation had failed to achieve its aim of disarming the Somali warlords, and had alienated the Somali people. For the past six months, the Americans have been looking after the Americans, seeking to minimise [*sic*] casualties. The UN should never be a military presence and a unilateral non-UN international military presence, be it the U.S. or anyone else working simultaneously."

Harper either wasn't aware of, or he failed to address, the fact that U.S. forces committed to Somalia were never given the mission to "disarm" Somali warlords regardless of the amount of emphasis given that objective by Boutros Boutros-Ghali. However, despite criticizing the U.S. role, Harper put his finger on one of the main flaws with multinational operations when he said: "The individual national units tended to operate in their own way and decide which bits and pieces of the UN mandate they would or would not implement and as a result, the UN military force never possessed the necessary level of coordination."

Harding concluded his report by pointing out that the UN military force was a "little more trigger-happy than they should have been in Somalia."

On Thursday, May 20th, Mohammed Farah Aidid returned in triumph to Mogadishu, thanking thousands of cheering supporters for defending it against foreign aggressors. He had spent the better part of the previous six months in Nairobi, Kenya, seeking international support and trying to arrange alliances with other Somali warlords.

This was not quite the ending envisioned by either President Bush or Clinton.

Chapter Ten

Cost, Closure and Clinton

The UN built an expensive, modern, American-style suburb in the middle of Mogadishu. A development of one hundred western style homes took shape with sewer, water, telephone, and power connections. Yet all of these trappings of civilization (complete with chilled chocolate milk and "Don't Drink and Drive" signs), remained out of reach of Somalia's 6.5 million citizens. The development was confined within the eighty-acre compound of the United Nations operation in Somalia (UNOSOM II) and it was well guarded.

The United Nations budgeted $1.6 billion (a large percentage of which was paid by American taxpayers) for its mission which was scheduled to expire in December, 1994. Of the money devoted to the military, UN officials in Mogadishu estimated that $72 million, or 4 percent, worked its way into the Somalian economy. Incredibly, even as one element of the UN command disbursed money to foreign contractors to build its compound with Western-style comforts, another section was planning how best to abandon what they had built in anticipation of the expiration of the UN mandate. Demonstrating his mastery of understatement, Richard W. Bogosian, senior U.S. diplomat in Somalia commented, "I'm not sure that we need to have developed things (in the compound) quite as much as they've been developed." A breakdown of the $639 million allocated for the November 1993 to May 1994 period offered a glimpse at UNOSOM's priorities. Almost $176 million was spent to hire the nineteen thousand UN soldiers posted to Somalia. Each soldier (except American military personnel)[27] collected $1.28 per day. Another $988 per soldier per month went to the governments that supplied the soldiers, with an additional bonus of $291 per month paid for each military specialist. As one UNOSOM official acknowledged, "If you have 5,000 Pakistani troops and Pakistan is collecting $1,000 a month for each of them, that's five million a month given to Pakistan alone." This is absurd, considering that UN countries have to be paid by the UN to participate, and American citizens foot the bill. At the same time, since the Clinton administration refused to class Somalia as a 'combat zone,' the troops were denied combat pay. Simultaneously, BAS/BAQ pay was deducted from their payrolls. The result was that deployment to Somalia cost them as much as $14 per day.

Then, of course, there was another $50.8 million budgeted for depreciation of the troops' equipment and vehicles, $33.4 million for food rations, and $23.5 million for the cost of sending troops home and bringing new soldiers to replace them. Other costs include $38.8 million to lease a fleet of helicopters and $20 million for ten airplanes. An extra $17.5 million was needed for spare parts for commercial and military vehicles. This amount did not include $3.5 million for gasoline, diesel, oil, and grease, $21 million for infrastructure repairs, and $4.5 million to operate UNOSOM's communications system, including a new digital switchboard and access to ten satellite earth stations.

The same UNOSOM official also said: "We've also got ideas for recreation, tennis and squash courts, swimming pool, and a mini-golf course, but we're not quite there yet. We don't want to be seen as looking after just ourselves when, after all, we're not going to be living here that long."

Incredibly with Somalia in arguably worse condition than it was before the UN arrived, at the end of March 1994, UNOSOM erected a new subdivision in the compound for eight hundred of its employees. It was on a newly-paved asphalt street named "Boutros-Boutros Alley." The new village cost about $12 million, including $7 million for the plumbing system. A UNOSOM team also bought $500,000 worth of furniture in Dubai.

UNOSOM hired more than 1,800 Somalis for everything from emptying out latrines to ditch digging. Yet the fact that the overwhelming majority of the money went to companies from elsewhere in the world rankled the Somalis. One UNOSOM official said, "We try to give them precedence as long as they're not totally stupid. If a Somali tells me he can build a bridge for $1,000, we tell him to get lost."

The UNOSOM headquarters was located on the site of the former U.S. embassy, a $35 million compound that was abandoned when the Siad Barre regime was overthrown in January, 1991. "We are like a consortium of investors," said a senior UN official. "How many quarters can we continue in the red without getting out? How long are we going to hurt and bleed?"

After all of the money spent, viewed from a helicopter Mogadishu possessed a "Road Warrior" quality to it.

Doorway to Hell

The UN staff in Mogadishu took care of themselves with the virtual blank check they'd been given to build a compound, while they complained to one another about their mission and their living conditions. Some of them were openly racist and would confide among themselves that the Somalis couldn't be trusted or govern themselves. The Somalis who were hired to work in the UN compound detected the racially superior attitude and resented it. More than one would work in the compound during the day and help man mortar crews at night that would lob rounds into the very area in which they'd been working.

Black UN officials were looked upon with suspicion. Leonard Kapungu, a Zimbabwean and chief political officer for the UN in Somalia said, "I would never delude anyone, there are guns and heavy weapons. It is not the peace I would want." Kapunga's office had to be repaired from the damage caused by a mortar round which had been zeroed in on it. Although many Somalis tended to defer to Kapunga because he was black, he was pragmatic about his evaluation. He observed, "Somalia is a classroom every day. It was a failed state, facing starvation and anarchy on an unprecedented scale. Not to have interceded would have meant that the world was a participant in genocide on a scale it wouldn't tolerate. Somalia would have been so weakened that it could have been co-opted by terrorist states.

"The problem for the world," he continued, "was how to save Somalia."

If the world wouldn't accept the losses of human life, apparently little consideration was given to what would happen in the United States when body bags were shipped home. The American commitment was made in spite of strong objections lodged by the American embassy in Nairobi, Kenya. The ambassador in Nairobi had a realistic appraisal for what the U.S. was going to get into and forwarded that evaluation to the State

Department. Unfortunately, overriding the ambassador's recommendation was the fact that the UN could not accomplish the mission without the help of the U.S. armed forces.

UN officials were disinclined to claim any marked success. Somalis, they asserted, were cynical, cooperating just enough to keep the UN cash cow flowing the hard currency they needed. To a great extent, they were correct. Somalia was very similar in many respects to the former Republic of Vietnam where there was always doubt about the South Vietnamese, whether they were true allies, VC or playing both sides simultaneously.

With the scheduled deactivation of UNOSOM in the spring of 1995, UNOSOM planners knew that it would take at least two hundred days to pack up and leave. That meant that the dismantling was scheduled to begin in September 1994, which ironically was also the same time the capital improvements were to be completed. Knowing that they were participating in a management nightmare, one UN official who demanded anonymity declared, "I am optimistic about the future of Somalia, but I am pessimistic about the ability of the UN." He had good reason to come to that conclusion. The UN was dependent upon a rich Uncle Sam. Without the support and involvement of the United States, virtually any major UN action in Somalia would be impotent and the U.S. had written off the UN experiment at imposing global world order over chaos.

In a period of American political history when debt plagued the U.S. economy, Somalia became an endless pit consuming American dollars.

The United States was the largest contributor to the United Nations in both direct and indirect costs. However, UN costs to American taxpayers for Somalia amounted to indirect expenditures. An analysis of costs for U.S. troops was reflective of the cost of any military involvement requiring deployments.

Doorway to Hell

As of January, 1994, the Department of Defense provided updated estimates of costs of its activities during the government's 1993 fiscal year which ends on September 30. The Department of Defense estimated that its incremental costs, those over and above the normal day-to-day operations in Somalia, totaled $887.5 million. By March 31, 1993, with all troops out of the country, the total incremental costs amounted to an estimated $1.6 billion.

The Department of Defense estimated that about $124.6 million of its costs would be reimbursed by the United Nations. However, DOD cost estimates and reimbursements do not include payments to the UN. Meanwhile the State Department estimated that the UN was expected to assess the U.S. an additional $58 million over the $158 million it had already required from U.S. taxpayers. So while Congress, executive branch departments, and the UN shuffled money from "pocket to pocket" in a shell game that prevented tracing of total accountability, the American taxpayer received only estimates on how much the Somalia operation cost depending upon who was asked and how precise the question was framed.

Richard Meyer writing for *Financial World* researched all available cost documents and stated: "Last year (1993) the United Nations was pouring over $2 million per day into the country. U.S. taxpayers were spending another $2.5 million a day to support our troop presence there."

To obtain a more digestible perspective, the calculated total costs for the 43rd Engineer Battalion (Heavy) for Operation Continue Hope was approximately $11,850,000. Since the cost of Operation Restore Hope was in the same range as Operation Continue Hope, deploying this one battalion twice cost the U.S. taxpayer over $23 million for two tours to Somalia. The 43rd Combat Engineer Battalion (Heavy) was admittedly a unique unit. It possessed an MTOE (Modification Table of Organization and Equipment) that contained an extraordinary amount of heavy equipment such as bulldozers, scoop-loaders, semitrailer trucks, cranes, floodlights, backhoes, extension booms, and trucks, along with many of the same items other battalions had. Those included weapons, highly-sophisticated and cost-intensive communications equipment, repair parts, and supplies.

By the time the last American forces left Somalia on March 25, 1994, more than 87,000 American soldiers, sailors, marines, and airmen had been sent to the Somalian theater or were in support of the operation, accompanied by ships, planes, vehicles, weapons, ammunition, and tons of supplies. While the Department of Defense seemed to have access to unlimited amounts of money for the operation under a defense budget calling for cuts across the board in all services, it managed to make up, at least in part, for expenditures on Somalia. It ordered cuts elsewhere in the defense budget, depleting the readiness of other units in the U.S. armed forces throughout the world.

What did the U.S. have to show for the investment? By the time the last UN official left Somalia, the country was a wreck. No authority existed beyond that which could be exerted by individual warlords in the regions they controlled. Economic activity was on a makeshift basis and subject to disruption by gunmen. No capital was available for investment and the sinking feeling that the 45 Americans who were lost in Somalia died in vain could not be shaken by an American public that increasingly looked upon the UN with skepticism.

On a smaller and more personal scale, despite all efforts to protect them from it, thirty-five soldiers from the 10th Mountain Division (L) were diagnosed with malaria after they returned to their home base at Fort Drum, New York. Most of them had

163

served in the Jubba River valley region of southern Somalia. Although the soldiers had taken mefloquine which prevented the most common form of malaria, and for four weeks after they returned home, mefloquine did not affect the vivax variety of parasite which attacked the thirty-five soldiers in New York.

There were other latent effects as well. For those who were married or related to the members of the 43rd Engineers, the second deployment was a particularly bitter pill to swallow. Other similar Engineer battalions hadn't gone at all, and yet their loved ones were marched through the "Doorway to Hell" a second time. It was as if they had already done their share, and then they were being sent back while others remained at home. Summing it up, LTC Davis commented, "It's the old story that when you accomplish more than your share of missions, you'll have more than your share of missions to accomplish."

There is an old axiom in the Army that the success or failure of any command is the direct and personal responsibility of the commander. That is a principle that has been proven throughout military history because every command reflects a commander's priorities and personality. The 43rd proved to be successful for several reasons, not the least of which was the fact that LTC Davis promised the families that his battalion would return when they finished their mission.

Meanwhile, Mrs. Davis, as the "first lady" of the battalion, pulled the families together into the "43rd Engineer Battalion Family Support Group" while the Battalion was deployed in both operations. Her involvement tended to provide a communications outlet for the worried family members and established a commonality among family members that was understood only by those associated with the 43rd. Family support groups became an asset to the families of deployed troops that developed two years before during the Persian Gulf

Doorway to Hell

War. Through satellite communications, LTC Davis was able to communicate messages to Fort Benning to a rear detachment. The rear detachment would then provide the most current unclassified information to Mrs. Davis who would then pass it along to the battalion's family members. In an environment where their loved ones were in the middle of the hottest spot in Somalia, such informal communications became a major contribution toward morale on the home front.

However, their contributions were principally internal. As far as the rest of the country was concerned, Somalia represented the classic example of where glory has a thousand fathers, humiliation is an orphan. When American forces returned home to a nation that despite Congressional resolutions lauding them for their success, was otherwise singularly parsimonious with expressions of appreciation for their efforts.

The comparison between treatment of American troops following the Persian Gulf war and that of those who returned from Somalia was nothing short of scandalous and insulting. The irony was that instead of civilian opposition when the veterans of Vietnam arrived home, those from Somalia encountered apathy on the part of their country. The returning veterans found an adverse command climate reflecting the desire on the part of the commander-in-chief to backpedal from Somalia as fast as possible. In fact, aside from the homecoming activities principally held by their posts and families, it almost seemed to some as if they were considered lepers by their own senior military leadership who got their career tickets punched two years before in the Persian Gulf.

This adverse climate generating from the highest political officials who were trying to disassociate themselves with anything connected to Somalia, manifested itself in a variety of adverse policy decisions.

165

Until troops in Somalia started coming under routine fire, military officials were proposing that Humanitarian Service medals be given to U.S. troops taking part in Operation Restore Hope. The awards were routinely given to those who assisted in the relief of Florida after Hurricane Andrew and are applicable to personnel who participate in a "significant military act" of a humanitarian nature. Except for the Air Force that awarded the medal to all crews of planes that touched ground at Mogadishu airport in transport of troops, food and supplies, the other services adopted another view.

In lieu of award of this medal, the Armed Forces Expeditionary Medal was authorized, however no Somalia campaign medal was authorized to indicate where the expedition took place, unlike the Persian Gulf of two years before[28]. To illustrate the issue even further, even though Somalia is adjacent to the Saudi Arabian peninsula, not even the Southwest Asia service medal was authorized for the Somalia veterans. As retired Army Colonel Harry Summers wrote, "What the military said loud and clear, to those who can read its somewhat arcane signals, is that peacekeeping humanitarian operations are in reality small-scale combat operations. And this has enormous significance.

"In the past, it has been the military that stood accused of deliberate obfuscation of the realities of war. It talked about `target servicing' when it meant blowing people and things to bits. It talked about `collateral damage' when it meant killing civilians who had the bad luck to be too close to a target.

"Words have consequences. A generation ago, social scientists blathered about how the United States needed to train soldiers in counterinsurgency to deal with revolution in the Third World. But the reality in the jungle was not the tools of

166

social science, but one infantry squad closing with another with fire and maneuver.

"Now some of these same people are talking about reorienting the military toward peacekeeping. But the reality in Somalia and Bosnia or Cambodia today is that before you can have peacekeeping, you must first have peacemaking. And that requires basic combat skills, which is why the decision on combat patches and on award of the Armed Forces Expeditionary Medal[29] was so important. They are evidence that senior military leaders understand the true nature of `peacekeeping humanitarian operations.' Would that the politicians and do-gooders understand it as well.

U.S. Central Command also adopted the position that valorous achievements under hostile fire were recognized by individual merit awards prior to June 5, 1993. The United States Marine Corps however, maintained that "*regardless of heroism demonstrated*", no valor awards would be approved for those who served in Operation Restore Hope. This was an incredible decision in view of the firefights Marines had engaged in with Somali gunmen during Operation Restore Hope. When heroism is intentionally ignored, it sets a tone for the future when service personnel will not know whether their sacrifices in blood and lives will be recognized by their own high command.

Secretary of the Army Gordon Sullivan authorized expanded wartime awards for soldiers who served in Somalia, but incredibly they were only applicable after June 5th. This determination, however, did not cover those who were in firefights during Operation Restore Hope. Recommendations for Bronze Stars were made by field commanders, but only a very few were approved despite the fact that Bronze Stars were handed out by the truckload after the Persian Gulf War[30].

167

Ironically, Bronze Stars may be awarded even in `peacetime' with the approval of the Secretary of the Army.

To receive the United Nations medal, ninety days or more of service in Somalia under United Nations command is required. An exception was made for members of the U.S. Quick Reaction Force who did not wear the blue beret of UNOSOM which included the 43rd. Initially, convoluted reasoning by desk-bound decision makers in the Pentagon specified that veterans of the Joint Task Force were not eligible because it was commanded by Army Major General Thomas Montgomery from December, 1992 through the UN assumption of command on May 4, 1993. Yet, throughout that period, the troops assigned to the JTF worked hand-in-hand with Canadian, Belgian, French, Italian, and numerous other UN forces. On September 15, 1993, the United Nations offered the UN medal for Somalia duty to eligible personnel who served under its command. However, the decision to accept this award was not forthcoming from U.S. Central Command because it was unwilling to solicit it for those who served in Somalia prior to May 5, 1993, during Operation Restore Hope.

It was obvious that the Clinton administration failed to understand the military culture due to their lack of experience in that culture by high ranking members of that administration. Awards and medals are vitally important to any military organization everywhere in the world. Armed forces personnel take the "measure" of one another not only by rank but by the decorations they wear. Morale and esprit-de-corps is directly related to what the French refer to as "Elan" that is the characteristic that motivates a military unit to perform under adverse, if not impossible conditions.

In addition to the parsimonious policy of providing such recognition, the U.S. Joint Chiefs of Staff rejected a request

168

from Central Command to allow American troops to draw pay supplements directly from the United Nations. The U.S. Foreign Assistance Act does not allow direct UN pay entitlement to American military personnel. Yet, according to the Department of Defense, the U.S. did receive a per soldier fee for GI's serving as part of the UN forces. Payment came from the UN Logistics Support command. According to Pat Richards of the Secretary of Defense Compensation Policy Directors Office, "This pay is primarily for Third World countries, to get them to participate." (Belgium, Canada, France, Germany, and Australia undoubtedly were fascinated to learn that the Office of the Secretary of Defense of the United States classified them as "third-world" countries).

Finally, military personnel deployed to Somalia, regardless of date, were not extended the Combat Zone Tax, an exclusion which would have exempted them from paying taxes on income earned during their tour of duty. There was plenty of precedent for such an exemption. Those who served during the Persian Gulf War were extended the tax benefit. To not extend the Combat Zone Tax exclusion in an environment where two Medals of Honor were issued was clearly indicative of a gross confusion in the administration as to what was really happening in Somalia.

Then again the presentation by President Clinton of posthumous Medals of Honor to the families of Master Sergeant Gary I. Gordon, Lincoln, Maine, and SFC Randall D. Shughart, Newville, Pennsylvania, who were killed during the Ranger raid when they tried to rescue CW4 Michael Durant was virtually forced by political circumstances.

The citations told the story of two heroic NCOs who "unhesitatingly volunteered to go to the aid of four wounded comrades at a second crash site despite being well aware of the

169

growing number of enemy personnel closing in." The citations told the story of Gordon and Shughart who fought their way through a maze of shacks and shanties and provided covering fire for an injured pilot "until their ammunition was depleted. After SFC Shughart was fatally wounded, MSG Gordon recovered a rifle from the crash site and gave it and the last five rounds of rifle ammunition to the injured pilot with the words, `Good Luck.' Then armed with his pistol, Gordon continued to fight until he was fatally wounded. By their extraordinary heroism, Sergeants Gordon and Shughart saved the pilot's life." The citations were submitted through the chain of command, but it wasn't until the White House learned from Democrat Senators on the Senate's Armed Services Committee that the surviving family members of the Ranger raid were going to criticize the administration's policy in Somalia during a scheduled appearance before a Congressional committee that the medals were presented.

Furthermore, when Clinton aides learned that Larry Joyce, the father of Army Sergeant Casey Joyce who bled to death waiting for medical aid during the Ranger raid in Mogadishu was planning to testify, the White House staff arranged a meeting with Clinton. The last minute meeting with Joyce and other surviving families became a political imperative when it was revealed that Joyce's testimony would constitute a bitter criticism of Clinton's leadership. Clinton and his advisors may have thought that such a meeting might soften the families' testimony. They were wrong.

Clinton met with the families in a 45-minute White House meeting, in which Mrs. Joyce broke down in tears. The next day Joyce told the Senate Committee that they should "Find out what role the President played in a foreign policy that is developed haphazardly and implemented by amateurs." The family members had heard Clinton's explanation that the raid was conducted without his knowledge. Joyce, a retired Colonel, asked the most obvious question, "Since the decision had already been made to pursue a diplomatic solution, why was the October 3rd raid launched?" He added, "Only days after the bloodbath, Clinton announced the withdrawal of all U.S. forces from Somalia."

James Smith of Long Valley, New Jersey who lost part of a leg in Vietnam as well as his son, Corporal James Smith, Jr. in the Ranger raid testified, "Doesn't he (the President) know what his people are doing? I think he said all the right schmoozing (sic) things, but I got the idea that he didn't have the slightest idea what was going on in Somalia. I do not want other loved ones to experience my grief because of a flawed foreign policy or a failure to support our troops in battle."

Barbara Cavaco, mother of Corporal James Cavaco declared, "They were sent in without adequate backup. It's just a real shame that an entire company was decimated because we have a secretary of defense who wasn't aware what the situation was." Colonel Joyce added, "Clinton had been avoiding us for months but suddenly an invitation emerged as soon as the White House was informed of the testimony the evening before the hearing." Mrs. Caroline Smith, the mother of Corporal Smith said, "Clinton spoke at length about the failures of the United Nations, but declined to accept any of the blame. It was always somebody else."

The families' testimony constituted a poignant assault on the Clinton administration's foreign policy in general and the Somalia policy in specific. Other testimony before the committee clearly established several other facts which were embarrassing to the Clinton administration and to the high command of Somalia. The Senators concluded the obvious that there was no unity of command, the top brass were divided and no one had the guts to stand up and sound off against bad policies. Furthermore, the hearings established that the raid was ordered by the administration and not by the United Nations, as Clinton had previously stated, and that Generals Colin Powell and Joe Hoar, commanding CENTCOM in Tampa, Florida had doubts about the raid which was ordered by Generals Montgomery and Garrison. Furthermore, the raid was ordered after the U.S. had lost 24 helicopters that had been shot down in and around Mogadishu before the raid. Why didn't Garrison cancel the raid because his troops didn't have the tools to do the job and the risk wasn't worth the gain? Both Montgomery and Garrison pushed the party line that armor wouldn't have made any difference and besides that it couldn't have gotten there in time[31]. What was obvious though that despite the spin placed on the party line before the Senate Armed Services Committee, it was tanks and armored personnel carriers that finally relieved the Rangers.

Major General Garrison, commander of the Special Operations Command publicly accepted responsibility for the raid and the losses. However, military personnel and political observers familiar with the military quickly declared that Garrison was being designated as the "fall guy" to cover the criticism that was being leveled at higher commanders and the administration. Despite the public sacrifice of the 49-year old Garrison, the fact that the entire operation was initiated without the knowledge of the commander-in-chief was the bottom line. As Colonel David Hackworth[32] later wrote, "If the President didn't know the biggest ground combat operation since Desert Storm was going down, our warriors and U.S. national security are in deeper trouble than I feared."

172

Doorway to Hell

Because of the political and media uproar created by the testimony, Clinton was forced during a press conference to defend his foreign policy against allegations that it was improvised from crisis to crisis. Carefully avoiding any mention of Somalia, he took credit for progress made in Russia and the former Soviet Republics and cited pressure placed on North Korea to dismantle nuclear weapons. This was little more than an attempt to finesse the subject that concerned the American people and impacted on Congress. The American people had come to the same conclusion as had Congress. Further commitment of American troops in conjunction with multinational forces, and especially with regard to ill-defined U.N. objectives, would be under much more restrictive conditions that would limit the President's options in the future.

Stung from the criticism of his foreign policy and the growing opposition in Congress, Clinton issued Presidential Decision Directive 25th on May 25th, 1994. The directive pulled U.S. forces back from what had been visualized as American troops assigned to a standing U.N. army for use in peacekeeping mission. The directive requires American policymakers to consider whether participation "advances American interests." Furthermore, such operations "should have a specified time frame tied to intermediate and final objectives and cost of participation. Vague and expanding objectives (mission creep) such as those that prevailed in Somalia would not be acceptable." Additionally, the directive requires that all future peacekeeping or peace enforcement operations be "well-organized, well-planned, and in the national interest of the United States."

When Clinton announced the new directive, it was immediately perceived as a reaction to the criticism and opposition that had mounted to his foreign policy and to the response Congress had received from the American people. Despite allies like Representative Ronald Dellums (D-CA)[33] who said, "Learning the lessons of Somalia is critically important because the United States and its military will be faced again and again with similar situations. Post-Cold War peacekeeping is a new, emerging area in which we have no experts. We are stumbling and fumbling to find our way in a world of breathtaking change. We need to learn how to engage in peacekeeping."

Such views which subordinated U.S. interests to those of the UN enraged many of Dellum's colleagues. Congressman Joel Hefley (R-CO) blasted Clinton, Aspin and Dellums for their incompetence by pointing out that "you don't stumble and fumble with the lives of American service personnel." Congressman Jim Ross Lightfoot (R-IA) told Madeline K. Albright, the U.S. representative to the United Nations, "You know, mothers and fathers are not anxious to have their sons and daughters go to war in some foreign country and die for something that they perceive we have no national interest in."

Underlying the reluctance to send loved ones into harm's way for fuzzy international objectives was a bone that stuck in the throat of the body politic. It was the fact that the commander-in-chief, while a student, not only admittedly avoided military service, but wrote that he "loathed" the military. The reaction of the American people was best expressed by a highly decorated Special Forces Vietnam Sergeant from Arkansas. He asked, "Can you tell me which Arkansas soldier's name is on the Vietnam Wall, who replaced Bill Clinton in the draft during Vietnam?"

Another example of the same view was published by nationally syndicated editorial writer Jim Wright, columnist of the *Dallas Morning News*. He wrote, "When those first flag draped coffins come off the ramps of the C-l30s, the TV cameras will be panning the dead kids and their uniformed pallbearers to the commander in chief who sent them in harm's way. While millions of another young generation were wearing those uniforms, Mr. Clinton was in England wearing radical hair and joining those who demanded that America make love not war. Faced with that scene of the homecoming dead, Americans will probably recall those old make "love not war" sloganeers and decide that what made sense for young Bill's political viability than (*sic*) makes sense for his foreign policy now; that crusades are one thing and meddling in other folks' tribal fights is quite another."

It was obvious that the Clinton administration, which just ten months previously began mapping a major role for the military in world peacekeeping, spreading democracy, and protecting human rights, had been forced into reassessing the military's suitability for such missions. Clinton indicated as much when during an October 14th press conference, he said, "When you talk about resolving long-standing disputes, the United States, as the world's only superpower, is no more able to do that than we were thirty or twenty years ago."

Others had similar observations. "The experience in Somalia has made us more cautious about using Americans in `peacekeeping' when there is any doubt about their safety," said Kathleen deLaski, Pentagon spokeswoman. Representative Jim Saxton (R-NJ) put it more bluntly, "The practice of sending U.S. troops to the world's trouble spots is a very dangerous foreign policy of minding other peoples' business." Baker Spring, a defense analyst for the Heritage Foundation underscored the issue in saying, "The heart of the problem is that we have U.S. forces involved in missions that are completely separate from U.S. interests." Clinton had been

175

given a political bloody nose over Somalia and he knew that it would not be as simple in the future to send U.S. troops into what might be harm's way, unless he could clearly articulate a specific objective that was achievable, perceived to be in the nation's strategic interest and was politically acceptable to the American electorate. It was now obvious, beyond those considerations, any commitment of American military forces undertaken in the future would be at considerable political jeopardy to any administration in power.

Chapter Eleven

The New World Disorder

Despite the armed opposition by the Somalian warlords, the casualties suffered during the entire operation, and the issue of two Medals of Honor, Somalia was never classified as anything but as "humanitarian peacekeeping." The President, by executive order, could have declared Somalia a combat zone, ensuring GIs' receiving all appropriate benefits and combat decorations.

Many civilian commentators and retired military personnel openly wondered if Clinton's failure to do so was more reflective of his anti-military attitude during his younger days as an antiwar student demonstrator than any specific policy decision he may or may not have made with regard to Somalia. On the other hand, if he felt that he had been "sandbagged" by President Bush at the last minute and wanted to rid himself of anything connected with Somalia, such actions or inactions on his part would still be reprehensible. The end result of these harshly interpreted policies and attitudes toward what became a politically unpopular operation shortchanged the veterans of Somalia.

Doorway to Hell

It is customary in the United States armed forces to analyze any past operation in the form of an after-action report. Always included is at least one section annotating "lessons learned" providing the benefit of the experience to others with like assignments in similar units. It is unfortunate that the same practice is not followed within the U.S. political spectrum which controls the military.

Pragmatic Americans would concede that the nation's interests must be served and defended in many parts of the world. Sometimes this means the nation must act alone, sometimes it is in coordination with allies or under operational control of an allied commander. However, in the past the command, employment, support, and ultimate security of American forces have always remained under American command, and missions were clearly defined. Language, supply, and equipment compatibility reasons kept this policy intact for three-quarters of a century.

Operation Restore Hope was perceived by many political and military leaders as a way to pioneer a new kind of American intervention policy, based on purely humanitarian reasons as far as the American people would be concerned. It was presented to the nation and the world as a credible action, since the U.S. allegedly had no strategic or economic interests in the region. The rationale the United States government used (as is the case when any government provides its citizens a reason for a military action) may not have represented all of the reasons that were within its realm of priorities.

"Humanitarian intervention" as a policy in Somalia was transparent at best and spurious at worst, in view of the condition of numerous other countries in Africa and elsewhere. Only the geographically and economically naive could believe that the U.S. did not have strategic military and economic interests in Somalia. Had Mihael Bukhanin, the 19th century Russian philosopher and historian been alive, he would undoubtedly have pointed to Somalia as an example of his conviction, "No one at all interested in the study of history could have failed to see that there was always some great material interest at the bottom of the most abstract, the most sublime and idealistic, theological and religious struggles."

It is inconceivable that President Bush and his advisors were ignorant of the geopolitical and economic significance of Somalia much less its value to U.S. military forces. That fact had been established a decade before the Somalian revolution through the presence of U.S. military forces at key points in that country. With a friendly government in power, an American military presence would not only help stabilize such a government and prevent it from being threatened by other powers, but also would enhance U.S. military power in the region. Such a positioning for U.S. forces would permit immediate deployment to critical areas of national strategic interest to the United States. The military option represented by Somalia was significant enough to warrant selection of that country as an intervention target.

From an economic perspective it is naive to believe that President Bush, who made his own personal fortune as a Texas oilman, was unaware of the increasing number of favorable geological analyses and seismic readings regarding the potential oil and gas production in the undeveloped Somalian strata. Anyone who read the annual reports of the American oil companies in the late 1980's would have learned that Americans were rapidly building refineries, purchasing drilling leases, and engaging in exploration activity. Just a cursory review of the abstracts of professional papers published over that decade would cause any prudent individual to come to the same conclusion as did the U.S. and world's oil industry. Aside from the unexplored areas of Siberia, the region lying from the southern tip of the Arabian peninsula, under the Red Sea, south through Somalia to the Kenyan border and off coast, represented potentially the world's second largest undeveloped oil and gas province. This huge oil field was in the initial stages of being explored and developed when the Somalian civil war erupted and interrupted operations. However, the oil reserves are still untouched and accessible to the first country that can make a deal with any stabilized Somalian government. The existence of those oil reserves will undoubtedly be on the agenda of any future government that finds some moral, political, military or humanitarian reason to inject itself into Somalia in the future.

Apart from the more obvious economic and military considerations, politically the multi-national operation was to have been the forerunner of a new kind of United Nations intervention policy that was articulated by Bush as a coming "New World Order." Such a policy would not require the traditional invitation from a host government. With UN approval, it would not carry the baggage of being intervention in another's country's internal affairs which prior to the UN was simple imperialism. The new approach was met with great enthusiasm by the Clinton administration. During the presidential campaign, Clinton endorsed Boutros-Ghali's idea of a "Rapid Deployment Force" of U.S. and other troops that would be "on call" to the UN Secretary General. No such force existed, but U.S. Ambassador-At-Large Strobe Talbott reflected administration thinking when he said, "The UN needs more power and resources for peacekeeping, including the ability to call on American troops to serve under the world body's flag."

Doorway to Hell

Another of Clinton's close advisors, Morton Halperin, urged then Secretary of Defense Les Aspin to make the Defense Department the instrument of "revolutionary policy" of international peacekeeping. A draft of a secret Presidential national security memorandum, drawn up in July 1993, rejected the rapid deployment force. However, it endorsed more than doubling the staff of the UN military headquarters in New York City, giving it an intelligence service, improved communications, and even a standing airlift capability.

Aspin told the Senate Armed Services Committee that the Clinton administration's commitment to the "UN's peacekeeping system is overextended." He continued, "Finding a way for nations to collectively deal with erupting violence will be one of the principal challenges facing the Clinton administration." What remained unclear, and what Aspin did not address, was what role the United States would or should play as a partner in multinational peacekeeping or peacemaking efforts. A more nagging problem facing the administration was that historically, the United States has been reluctant to send its troops into military operations under foreign commanders.[34]

"It has to do with the way we feel about our troops," a senior Pentagon spokesman explained. "Military leaders fear that under foreign leadership, U.S. troops could be in more jeopardy than they would be under a U.S. commander. They could get into situations where they are not properly supported, where they don't have enough firepower or air support when they needed it. In addition, UN forces often operate under very restrictive Rules of Engagement that could endanger U.S. troops. In some operations, UN rules have permitted troops to fight only when attacked. In others, the only weapons they have been permitted to carry have been side arms."

Doorway to Hell

The UN policy of arming lightly and of limited response contrast to the U.S. military's policy of not getting involved in military action unless it does so with overwhelming force. The strongest advocate of this approach was none other than General Colin Powell, the Chairman of the Joint Chiefs of Staff who despite political pressure to do so, refused to moderate that view.

The UN's record of success is not encouraging said Andrew Cowin, a defense analyst for the Heritage Foundation. The post-Soviet collapse explosion of violence throughout the world focused attention on the UN to do something about it. Since 1988, the UN has undertaken 14 peacekeeping operations which is more than it attempted in the previous 40 years.

Aspin underscored the growth of UN involvement. He said, "The UN peacekeeping budget has skyrocketed from $700 million in 1991 to $2.8 billion in 1992. It is also clear that much more than traditional peacekeeping operations are required." Where UN troops used to monitor ceasefires, they have converged into a force being sent in to hostile areas to disarm warring factions and bring stability to countries, the populations of which resent their presence.

Operationally, there is concern that the United Nations is ill-suited in terms of its own command structure for managing military operations. At the Security Council level one of the permanent members can veto any military action. At the troop level, questions remain as to what the soldier is supposed to do if given an order from a foreign commander that is in the soldier's view, immoral or illegal. Clashes of cultures and maintenance of discipline have the potential for operational disaster.

The political problem of subjecting American troops to foreign command is the one that bothers political leaders most.

Doorway to Hell

A pentagon spokesman said, "Remember, the President has to answer to American families if U.S. troops are misused or killed while under foreign commanders."

Although Clinton initially signaled his willingness to consider assigning American troops to a standby UN force, in contrast to President Bush's policy that ruled out such an option, as the Somalian adventure grew more chaotic Clinton recognized that U.S. troop involvement in UN operations was a political minefield. Intending to assert U.S. authority over deployment of American troops and dissuade the world body into presuming that the U.S. armed services represented an extension of UN power, Clinton informed the UN General Assembly that the United States would be asking hard questions about future UN missions: "Does the proposed mission have clear objectives? Can an end to it be identified? How much will the mission cost?"

Clinton's remarks were widely hailed as a signal of retreat from his previous position described as "globalism." In fact, they did not. President Clinton was attempting to be all things to all people. While he sounded tough on the criteria U.S. troops would be committed, he simultaneously reiterated his administration's support for: "A genuine UN peacekeeping headquarters with a logistics unit that can be deployed on a moment's notice."

This philosophical approach by the President ignored the value of unity of command among indigenous forces. In actuality, the fundamental weakness of such an approach had already been clearly demonstrated in Somalia. This was recognized by Colonel Kenneth Allard when he wrote, "There should be no mistaking the fact that the greatest obstacles to unity of command during UNOSOM II were imposed by the United States on itself."[35]

Doorway to Hell

Yet, even as the dead from the October 1993 Ranger raid were being counted and public furor was rising, Clinton's Deputy Ambassador to the United Nations was voting to send more American troops on another ill-defined peacekeeping mission to war-torn Rwanda. A tiny, land-locked nation in the heart of Africa, Rwanda has no geographic, strategic, or economic value to the United States. The action did have political value to Clinton. He needed the thirty-eight votes of the "Black Caucus" in the House of Representatives to support his health and crime bills, and they were claiming "racism" as being the reason the U.S. did not intervene in Haiti or Rwanda.

This action on the part of the Clinton administration clearly pleased Boutros-Ghali because it supported his agenda. As the Communist empire collapsed, Boutros-Ghali declared the new era to be an extraordinary opportunity to expand the UN's peacekeeping role, and he set out to make the most of it.

Unlike most Americans, the Clinton foreign policy team displayed a deep-seated reluctance to have America act as a great power in its own interests. Simultaneously, however, it mustered substantial enthusiasm for deploying U.S. forces in multi-national adventures. The Clinton administration designed a foreign policy that was purged of national interest then stuffed with a fuzzy multinationalism.

Jeane Kirkpatrick, the highly-respected former U.S. Ambassador to the United Nations wrote: "Americans have no problem with multilateral action if it is in accord with American purposes and if U.S. forces are well-armed, supplied, and commanded, as when the President orchestrated the allied effort in the war against Iraq. But Clinton's U.N. enthusiasts envision American troops marching to aid vague global interests that are remote from American ideals.

Doorway to Hell

"President Clinton, not U.N. Secretary General Boutros Ghali is commander-in-chief of American armed forces. He would do well to learn the lessons of Somalia: that the U.N. Secretariat is not competent to command military operations, nor did the U.N. charter ever authorize such a role for that office. Furthermore, an American president cannot delegate to the U.N. his constitutional responsibility for the direction and leadership of the nation's armed forces."

From a less-partisan view, Patrick Glynn, a resident scholar at the American Enterprise Institute wrote: "We now surely know that justifying intervention on the grounds of military `do-ability' as defined by the Pentagon is no substitute for political leadership, and strategic clarity."

Any impartial analysis of the stated or presumed reasons for the U.S. commitment to Somalia will eventually be more thoroughly determined with the more impartial perspectives that the passage of time affords, along with availability to memoirs and documents not presently accessible. One thing did result from the intervention that was unexpected, especially by President Clinton. He had once remarked that he wanted to spend no more time on foreign affairs than absolutely necessary, because he had been elected to force the pace of domestic change. That statement could stand for his earlier approach to foreign affairs in general. Somalia may have cured him of his belief that he could get by keeping half an eye on foreign policy at odd moments. (On the other hand, it may not have had any effect at all. He later approved the commitment of American air power and U.S. troops to Bosnia and Macedonia, while he was committing his energies and focus to the proposed national health plan that was beaten back by Congress.)

Of the lessons learned in Somalia, possibly the most profound was that the American people developed a pronounced

185

reluctance to mount or join any peacekeeping operation except one that poses little or no risk to American service personnel. They have made that abundantly clear to Congress. When Congress got the message, as is often the nature of politicians, they began to look for scapegoats and turned their attention toward television's coverage of the conditions in Somalia prior to the intervention.

Even Boutros-Ghali complained that American television coverage was making his life "more miserable than it already was." Approaching the issue, "Is television forming foreign policy in the new age?" the House Foreign Affairs Committee held an extraordinary session of hearings during the week of April 22nd, 1994. Appearing before the committee were numerous "star" witnesses. These included news commentator Ted Koppel of ABC who testified: "When a policy and its consequences have not been adequately explained, an informational vacuum is created that gives an even greater resonance to those who bear no real responsibility for carrying out U.S. foreign policy."

Supporting Koppel's testimony was that of historian Michael Beschloss who pointed out that (due to television) "presidents have less flexibility in deciding how to respond to international crises." Ed Turner, vice president of CNN also testified: "We at CNN do not consider the impact of our proposed coverage on policy, the U.S. or any other country...If we began to attempt to figure in foreign policy, the organization would wind up in a swamp of "what ifs" and "maybes."

Yet there were those who discarded the impact of television and suggested a completely different reason for the Somalian incursion. As Georgie Ann Geyer, a nationally-syndicated columnist pointed out on April 29, 1994: "There was no American public outcry at all that was forcing the Bush administration into Somalia. Indeed, the pictures of human beings being slaughtered in Bosnia were far worse, and far more persistent, than were those in Somalia. Officials (in the Bush administration) moved to feed Somalia so that they would not have to intervene in Bosnia, believing that an "easy" intervention in Somalia, would take the attention from a potential military quagmire such as Bosnia."

Whether or not one or more of these reasons constituted a hidden agenda is debatable. What did emerge from the Somalian experience was a growing doubt among the American people as to the advisability and desirability of U.S. involvement in UN operations consisting of more than simply "human- itarianism" or some other ill-defined goal.

It would be a supreme irony if the bravery, valor, and heroism of American forces in Somalia require U.S. leaders to become more isolationist than globalist in their perspectives. Spurring such thought were intellectuals such as *Atlantic Monthly* contributing editor Robert D. Kaplan, author of *Balkan Ghosts*, who commented in the *Washington* Post, "Ultimately, the reorganization of our foreign policy toward broad population and environmental programs, fortified here and there with rare, well-timed military interventions, will define the post-Cold War arena. As upheaval becomes planetary, the region of the globe that combines a high level of human development with an idealistic sense of mission will lead the battle to stamp out the new age primitivism. We will either lead, or we may fall victim to the same demons."

Yet, the result of the operations in Somalia tended to crystallize in the mind of Americans something far more fundamental than mere esoteric ideals. Despite intellectual appeals to the contrary, those delegated the management of international affairs by a disinterested chief executive were forced to "gear down" their headlong rush to make "globalism" a new "world order." It also compelled Clinton to re-examine his priorities. The U.S. House of Representatives and one-third of the U.S. Senate, facing reelection in less than a year, began demanding an answer to the question, "What interventions are in the strategic interests of the United States?" If foreign policy is based on the answer to that question alone, Somalia might have been justified although the American people would not have known since "humanitarianism" was the only reason used for the intervention.

Without demanding a pragmatic answer to the strategic interest question, the American people might otherwise be confronted with a policy wasting the nation's resources and lives of its service personnel in military operations accomplishing little. Continuation of such interventions might weaken the United States both in terms of will and capability. This weakening process could increase the nation's susceptibility to foreign pressure, both economic and diplomatic, upon future generations.

Presuming that events have forced a dogmatic administration to become more pragmatic, the forty-five Americans will not have lost their lives in vain. Their sacrifice may have temporarily stalled the globalists' drive toward a "New World Order." Furthermore, the sight of body bags being sent home from a "humanitarian" operation caused Americans to demand answers from political leaders who had initially appeared willing to sacrifice the next generation for the UN's "international goals."

Of all of the issues though that rose to the surface of the Somalia cauldron, subordination of U.S. troops to UN command would not go away. Such subordination causes significant problems for U.S. military personnel. For example, no American soldier is expected to carry out what he regards as an illegal order. If an American soldier refuses to obey such an order, is he subject to American law under the UCMJ[36], or can he simply be shot for mutiny on the spot by some Russian, South Korean, or Turkish commander who would regard such action as within his rights?

Furthermore, those who maintain that the U.S. should move away from its unilateral security efforts and place its forces under the UN flag are not those who would serve in such a command. Imagine having to ask a Pakistani forward observer for supporting fire who would then have to forward the request through a Polish Fire Direction Control Center, calculate it on Japanese built computers, and send the order to a Russian artillery battery.

The fact is that multinational forces are simply unable to coordinate military actions at the level when they become engaged in a serious combat situation and lives are being lost. That is a far cry from the small UN Middle East observer missions that have been underway for years and function under UN command. Because of these small successes, key UN officials, with the agreement of Clinton appointees, established as one of their objectives the placing of national military forces under UN commanders in all UN military actions.

The concept that UN military decisions may be made by commanders from nations whose military forces are relatively ineffective, but whose decisions will place American forces in jeopardy, is a political disaster for a future American administration waiting to happen. The idea of military officers from some third-world country whose troops are used to living on raw fish and rice balls, commanding U.S. personnel and making life and death decisions for them, wouldn't last past the next off-year Congressional election.

Doorway to Hell

Coordinating and working with disparate allied forces is a nightmare when lives are being lost. The military forces of different nations may be participating under different mandates and have different views of what their purpose and charter is. In Somalia, 27 nations deployed their forces. Clearly the ad-hoc UN coalition arrangements became a recipe for disaster.

In Somalia, tensions and disputes arose between allied forces, specifically between the U.S., French, Italians, Pakistanis, and Malaysians. The Nigerians were also angry at the Italians whom they believe did not come to their aid when they were under attack. Combat is not the best time to discover that your allies are undependable.

Compounding the foregoing problems, military intelligence is by definition close-held and primarily for the commander's use. Furthermore, decisions to take military action, such as in the Ranger raid in Mogadishu, are also often classified for obvious reasons. Virtually all nations have no way of knowing how secure other country's military forces are with reference to any shared intelligence, or how effective their counter-intelligence might be. Multinational forces tend to function in their own vacuum of information generated by themselves. As a result, any military operation without close coordination among supporting units is limited to the scope of the committed units only. To achieve that coordination, intelligence must be shared which if compromised might result in the loss of sources. Few military intelligence officers worth the name would trust a foreign nation with their own generated intelligence.

The independent actions of ill-disciplined allied forces in a multinational role tend to complicate an already tenuous situation. The attack of Pakistani troops on non-combatants raised the level of hostility in Somalia against all UN forces, including Americans. Such independent actions can often change

190

the environment and entire mission inadvertently because of the impact they may have.

The difficulty of dealing with such changing conditions for the average American GI is why the court martial conviction of U.S. Army MP Specialist Fourth Class James Mowris was overturned by the commander of Fort Carson, Colorado. The Commander, General Guy A.J. LaBoa set aside the conviction in October, 1993 after reviewing the case. It had already become evident that civilian casualties will result if hostilities erupt during peacekeeping missions. The U.S. media and public are very sensitive to such casualties. But, U.S. military personnel are trained for combat, not for peacekeeping or peace enforcement against guerrilla forces such as in Somalia, and they will react according to their training and protect themselves. In the process, they will generate political and public criticism for inflicting casualties on civilians and creating political incidents that American governments may find intolerable.

Despite all of these very real pragmatic obstacles to such arrangements, in 1993 a draft proposal of a Presidential Decision Directive written by the Clinton administration was leaked prematurely which proposed to make official a directive to the Department of Defense to prepare to place U.S. forces under UN commanders. It was of little wonder to his political opponents as well as many professional military personnel, that such a directive would generate out of an administration led by an individual who not only avoided military service himself, but "loathed"[37] the military as an anti-war, demonstrator and student at Oxford[38].

Less than a month after the last American troops left Somalia, President Clinton appeared to not have learned anything from the experience.

Doorway to Hell

In speaking to the American people, Clinton attempted to explain why American pilots had been assigned to bomb Serbian positions in Bosnia. His words, as pointed out by Jeane Kirkpatrick, former UN ambassador, had a "Who me?" quality as if he were describing an action for which he had no responsibility. Clinton justified his actions with the statement, "This is a clear expression of the will of NATO and the will of the United Nations. We have said we would act if we were requested to do so. We have done so and we will do so again if we are requested." His comments were framed almost as if the U.S. had no role in the decision making processes of either NATO or the UN. The fact is that neither NATO or the UN could operate without U.S. participation and support.

Clinton's rationale was reflective of the opinion of many members of his administration that the UN Security Council was the only institution that could legitimatize the use of force. According to such an internationalist view, the great nations of the world should renounce the unilateral use of force and reduce their armed forces. Only multinational forces should address the threat of some outlaw nation. It is a position that makes legitimacy dependent upon a single veto of any permanent member such as China. It is this vision of international sanctions that inspired Presidential Decision Directive 13 which is supposed to deal with the criteria for peacekeeping. Under such a philosophical approach, reaction to future war and aggression will be dealt with by "peacekeeping."

When Secretary of Defense William Perry replaced Aspin, many thought there was a possibility the momentum toward global multinationalism would change. Perry took greater control of the Department of Defense and displayed the capability to reorient the department's planning and direction. Those who had such preconceptions would be sadly disappointed when they read an essay written by Perry in 1992. Entitled "Military Action: When to Use It and How to Ensure Its Effectiveness" which was included in the book "Global Engagements" is a clear statement of support for renouncing American forces in favor of a policy of "global engagement." Obviously, the globalists in power were not about to allow anyone else into their circle who did not support their view.

The crises that Americans will endure in the attempt on the part of internationalists to use American troops for their own ends have not ended. The one-world social-globalist perspective will continue until the administration is changed by the American electorate. Even then, there will be some, like dormant cancer cells, left buried in the Washington infrastructure who will be waiting for another chance to convert American power to one-world UN power.

Those who do so weren't in Somalia or anyplace like it, and they will ensure that their sons and daughters don't go either.

Chapter Twelve

Lessons Learned

From May 9-21, 1994, a group of seventy-three flag and field-grade officers and civil servants gathered at the U.S. Army Peacekeeping Institute, U.S. Army War College, Carlisle Barracks, Pennsylvania to consider the lessons the Army learned from its Somalian experience. Representatives of the other services and the Joint Staff also took part in the meeting convened by MG Thomas Montgomery, the senior U.S. commander in Somalia from March, 1993 to March 1994.

Formally titled as the Somalia After Action Review Committee, it was informally dubbed "The Montgomery Board" and divided into three panels. One panel examined how UN policy relating to peace enforcement affected U.S. operations. The second panel investigated command-and-control issues, and the third examined the effect of Somalia-like missions on how the Army mans, equips, trains, and structures its forces.

The Montgomery Board's findings were delivered to Defense Secretary William Perry in June and consisted of an executive summary and a detailed "lessons learned" section organized in a "problem-discussion-recommendation" format. To avoid "ruffling bureaucratic feathers" recommendations that referred specifically to policy areas above the Army level were called observations." Several of the observations developed by the Montgomery Board will undoubtedly lead to changes in the Army's urban operations doctrine.

The Board found that there is a fine line between leaving a unit in country long enough to become streetwise and put that institutional knowledge to good use, and leaving it in so long that morale begins to suffer. As noted by Colonel Robert Barefield, Director of Plans for the XVIII Airborne Corps based at Fort Bragg, North Carolina, "You don't want to beat a unit to death and keep it there too long; the other side of it is there is a learning curve." He continued, "Over six months is probably counterproductive."

MG Montgomery pointed out that previous assumptions regarding the ineffectiveness of armor supporting light infantry in an urban environment were not valid. "Armor can play an important role in urban combat," Montgomery said.

Tasked with studying lessons learned from Somalia, one officer observed that "realistic live fires (training exercises) pay off." His point was that units that ready themselves for peacekeeping operations in urban terrain by conducting such exercises will be better prepared for action "when the bullets start flying for real."

A critical issue that was identified included the lack of effective military intelligence in the Somalian environment. Colonel Barefield noted that because of the initial mission of securing humanitarian relief routes, effective intelligence was available only from agents. Furthermore, Somalia's clan-based society was difficult for Western intelligence agencies to penetrate, and this dearth of information became a critical issue for U.S. forces as the mission there heated up.

Helicopter employment tactics will adjust to urban warfare in the future if the Montgomery Board's findings are heeded. Marine Colonel Matthew Broderick, Commander of the 24th Marine Expeditionary Unit, said that at the height of the fighting with Mohammed Aidid's forces during the Ranger raid in October, "they were shooting up to 120 to 150 RPGs (Russian-designed, shoulder-mounted, anti-tank RPG-7 rocket-propelled grenades) at once" at the Blackhawk helicopters. The losses of three UH-60 Blackhawks to RPG fire brought home the underestimated threat posed by RPGs fired in salvos at low-flying helicopters. One expert said, "You always are going to take some kind of casualties if you've got that many people shooting at you." The solution would be to fly low and fast or high and out of range and to vary flight patterns continuously.

When retired U.S. Navy Admiral Jonathan Howe offered $25,000 for Aidid, payable to any Somali who helped turn Aidid in for arrest by the United Nations, there were no takers. MG Montgomery said ten months later, "I'd have put a million dollars on the table instead of $25,000." The point made was that in a city brutally controlled by Aidid and his supporters who mutually hated the UN, the Montgomery Board concluded that in the future if a native is going to be asked to risk his life, the incentive offered had better be worth the risk.

Finally, concern over "collateral damage" should not take priority over allowing a U.S. soldier to shoot if he feels his life is directly at risk. "If an American soldier feels his life is threatened by a guy raising a weapon he has a right to shoot," MG Montgomery said. "We don't want the soldiers to be timid. If you became timid in Somalia you become dead."

Doorway to Hell

Because of the restrictions on the Montgomery Board, some of the lessons learned that applied to the political spectrum were not articulated. The most devastating indictment of the mistakes made in Somalia were not pronounced by columnists, historians, writers, commentators or soldiers. The clearest articulation of the evaluation of what happened in Somalia, and their opinion of the Clinton administration in general was handed in by the American people during the November off-year elections of 1994.

Four months before that decision was rendered, and a month after the Montgomery Board adjourned to issue its findings; on June 30, 1994, the flags, battle streamers and company guidons of the 43rd Engineer Combat Battalion (Heavy) were furled and packed away for the last time.

After three-quarters of a century of service, the Battalion was formally deactivated during stand-down ceremonies at Fort Benning, Georgia. Commanding the final formation was LTC Robert L. Davis, and comprising it were the remaining officers and troops who had not yet been reassigned to other commands or whose orders would be effective upon the 43rd's inactivation. Also present were several General Officers, former Battalion Commanders and Command Sergeants Major who had traveled to Fort Benning for the occasion.

After the speeches were over, the awards given, and the final review conducted, the 43rd's colors were furled and covered, to be returned to the Department of the Army for storage. LTC Davis dismissed the final formation, and the 43rd Engineer Combat Battalion (Heavy) passed into the military history of the United States Army.

As the members of the 43rd shook hands and said farewell prior to departing for their next destinations, it was a melancholy time for many of the experienced and hardened

197

veterans of the Battalion. As they left the Fort Benning Parade Ground, they retained the consolation of knowing that together they helped write their own special chapter in the history of two nations.

A passage in Shakespeare's Henry V best reflects what these troops would feel about the missions they performed and the men and women with whom they shared danger and hardship in Somalia, East Africa in 1993:

> "And gentlemen in England now a-bed, Shall think themselves accursed they were not here, And hold their manhoods cheap whiles any speaks, That fought with us upon Saint Crispin's day."

Whether some of them would openly admit it or not, the sentiments expressed in that passage would bind them together for the rest of their lives. They were members of the only American military command that marched through the "Doorway to Hell"--twice.

On September 1st, 1994, the remaining members of the American diplomatic mission lowered the U.S. flag from its flagpole on the former U.S. embassy and departed Somalia. This action was followed by a United Nations Security Council vote to withdraw all U.N. forces from Somalia by January 1, 1995. The justification was that due to increasing hostility to the U.N. and intensity of clan fighting, the remaining forces were unable to establish or maintain any semblance of order.

Somalia was finally left to its own destiny.

Chapter Thirteen

On Behalf Of The President, We Regret To Inform....

Of all of the assignments that a Soldier, Sailor, Airman or Marine can be ordered to perform, the most emotionally gut-wrenching is to serve on a Casualty Notification Team. Members of the service to which the casualty belonged, accompanied often by a service chaplain, are called upon to seek out the nearest relative and provide official notification of the death of the loved one. Unlike World War II, when a simple telegram served such a function, the service personnel assigned that mission in the modern armed forces have to bear the emotional brunt of the shock displayed by the parents, spouse, or other family member designated as the NOK (Next Of Kin). Including fourteen who were killed in accidents, by the time the last American troops withdrew from Somalia on March 25th, 1994, notification teams had to inform forty-three American service-connected families and the families of two civilians that their men had lost their lives in Somalia.

It is to those forty-five, and the unselfish valor and courage they displayed, that this book is dedicated.

KIA (Killed In Action)

(Civilian) Lawrence L. Freeman, 51
Fayetteville, NC
December 23, 1992

PFC Domingo Arroyo, 21
Elizabeth, NJ
January 12, 1993

LCpl Anthony D. Botello, 21
Wilburton, OK
January 26, 1993

SFC Robert H. Deeks, 40
Littleton, CO
March 3, 1993

SP/4 Mark E. Gutting, 25
Grand Rapids, MI
August 8, 1993

SGT Christopher K. Hilgert, 27
Bloomington, IN
August 8, 1993

SGT Ronald N. Richerson, 24
Portage, IN
August 8, 1993

Doorway to Hell

SP/4 Keith D. Pearson, 25
Tavares, FL
August 8, 1993

PFC Matthew K. Anderson, 21
Lucas, IA
September 25, 1993

SGT F. C. Richardson, 27
Sunnymead, CA
September 25, 1993

SGT Eugene Williams, 26
Chicago, IL
September 25, 1993

CWO Donovan L. Briley, 33
North Little Rock, AR
October 3, 1993

SSG Daniel D. Busch, 25
Portage, WI
October 3, 1993

CPL James M. Cavaco, 26
Foretdale, MA
October 3, 1993

SFC Earl R. Fillmore, Jr., 28
Blairsville, PA
October 3, 1993

Doorway to Hell

CWO Raymond A. Frank, 45
Monrovia, CA
October 3, 1993

MSG Gary L. Gordon, 33
Lincoln, ME
September 25, 1993

SGT James L. Joyce, 24
Denton, TX
October 3, 1993

PFC Richard W. Kowalewski, Jr., 20
Crucible, PA
October 3, 1993

PVT James H. Martin, Jr., 23
Collinsville, IL
October 3, 1993

MSG Timothy Martin, 38
Aurora, IN
October 3, 1993

SP4 Dominick M. Pilla, 21
Vineland, NJ
October 3, 1993

SGT Lorenzo M. Ruiz, 27
El Paso, TX
October 3, 1993

Doorway to Hell

SFC Randall D. Shughart, 35
Newville, PA
October 3, 1993

SP4 James E. Smith, 21
Long Valley, NJ
October 3, 1993

CWO Clifton P. Wolcott, 36
Cuba, NY
October 3, 1993

SSG William D. Cleveland, Jr., 34
Peoria, AZ
October 4, 1993

SGT Thomas J. Field, 25
Lisbon, ME
October 4, 1993

SFC Matthew L. Rierson, 33
Nevada, IA
October 6, 1993

SGT Cornell Houston, 31
Compton, CA
October 7, 1993

(Civilian) Kai Lincoln, 23
(UN Worker) New York City, NY
November 13, 1993

Non-Battle Deaths

PVT Daniel J. Conner, 29
Huntington Beach, CA
February 15, 1993

PVT Don D. Robertson, 28
Tustin, CA
March 2, 1993

L/Cpl William A. Rose, 20
San Joaquin, CA
March 6, 1993

PVT Daniel L. Harris, 21
Newsom, VA
March 18, 1993

SP4 Edward J. Nicholson, 21
Houston, TX
October 6, 1993

L/Cpl Jesus Perez, 20
San Antonio, TX
December 15, 1993

SSG Brian P. Barnes, 26
Cole Camp, MO
March 14, 1994

Doorway to Hell

TSG Robert L. Daniel, 34
Gray, GA
March 14, 1994

MSG Roy S. Duncan, 40
Miami, FL
March 14, 1994

SSG William C. Eyler, 32
Tulsa, OK
March 14, 1994

CPT David J. Melhop, 30
Zellwood, FL
March 14, 1994

SSG Mike E. Moser, 32
Mt. Ayr, IA
March 14, 1994

CPT Mark A. Quam, 27
Madison, WS
March 14, 1994

CPT Anthony R. Stefanik, Jr., 31
Johnstown, PA
March 14, 1994

Missing In Action (MIA)

(Civilian) Alfred Peters, 36,
(Water and Sanitation Engineer, American Red Cross)

Epilogue

After the colors were furled...

COL Phillip Anderson
Commander, 36th Engineer Group
Operation Restore Hope--Selected for promotion to the rank of Brigadier General and assigned as the Deputy Commanding General of the Army's Engineer School at Fort Leonard, Wood, Missouri.

LTC Robert L. Davis
Commander, 43rd Engineer Combat Battalion (Heavy)
Operations Restore Hope and Continue Hope--Selected by the Department of the Army as one of 16 U.S. Army Engineer officers for senior military schooling in 1994. He was transferred from Fort Benning, Georgia, and assigned as a student at the prestigious United States Air War College, Montgomery, Alabama.

MAJ Mark Feierstein
S-4, 36th Engineer Group
Operation Restore Hope--S-3, 43rd Engineer Combat Battalion (H) - Operation Continue Hope--Assigned as the S-3, 36th Engineer Group, Fort Benning, Georgia and later posted to duty in the Netherlands.

MAJ Allen C. Estes
S-3, 43rd Engineer Combat Battalion (H)
Operation Restore Hope--Transferred from S-3, 36th Engineer Group to the University of Colorado, for the purpose of pursuing a PhD education program. He was then assigned to assume the duties of a professor on the faculty of the United States Military Academy, West Point, New York as a newly promoted Lieutenant Colonel.

CPT (MD) Brian Unwin
Battalion Surgeon - 43rd Engineer Combat Battalion (H)
Operation Restore Hope--Promoted to Major-Medical Corps, initially assigned as Flight Surgeon Aviation Medicine, Fort Benning, and then transferred to Fort Gordon, Georgia as an Instructor on the Family Practice Residency Staff, Eisenhower Army Medical Center.

CPT (CH) Dale Forrester
Chaplain, 43rd Engineer Combat Battalion (H)
Operation Restore Hope--Assigned to the Chaplain staff of the U.S. Army Infantry Center Fort Benning, Georgia, and promoted to Major.

CPT Jeffrey T. Bochonok
S-1, (Personnel/Admin), 43rd Engineer Combat Battalion (H)
Operation Continue Hope--Following inactivation of the 43rd, he was assigned initially to the S-3 Section, 36th Engineer Group, and later assumed command of the 63rd Engineer Company, Fort Benning, Georgia.

1LT Brian E. Wheeler
Signal Officer, 43rd Engineer Combat Battalion (H)
Operations Restore Hope and Continue Hope, Upon return to Fort Benning, he was transferred to the position of Computer Automation Officer, 36th Engineer Group. After installing a wide area computer network. Later while attending the the Signal Officers Advanced School, Fort Gordon, Georgia he was presented the Meritorious Service Medal for his service in Somalia. After completing a successful tour as Commander of Headquarters Company, 86th Signal Battalion, 11th Signal Brigade, he resigned his commission in 1997 to attend the University of Oklahoma School of law, where he graduated with honors in 2000. At present he is serving as a federal staff attorney for the Honorable H. Dale Cook, Senior U.S. District Judge for the Northern U.S. District of Oklahoma, and serves as a Captain in the USAR Judge Advocate General Corps.

CSM Lawrence Maxwell
Command Sergeant Major - 43rd Engineer Combat Battalion (H), Operations Restore Hope and Continue Hope-- Transferred from Fort Benning, Georgia to assume the duties of Command Sergeant Major of the 84th Engineer Combat Battalion (Heavy), Schofield Barracks, Hawaii.

SFC Osieo Lopez
Communication Chief/NCO- 43rd Engineer Combat Battalion (H), Operation Restore Hope--Following Operation Restore Hope, SFC Osieo Lopez returned to his parent unit at Fort Hood, Texas.

Authors' Note

Awards and recognition to the veterans who served in Somalia, East Africa during Operations Restore and Continue Hope were parsimonious at best. Unusually arbitrary and restrictive interpretations were placed on eligibility requirements for valor and meritorious service awards that were routinely issued two years before to Persian Gulf War veterans. LTC Robert L. Davis, Commander- 43rd Engineer Combat Battalion (H). Davis led a total of more than a thousand of his engineers into a hostile fire theater twice, achieved his unit's mission with distinction, and returned without the loss of a single soldier. Yet a recommendation for the Bronze Star (one that can be awarded with approval of the Secretary of the Army in peacetime) was denied because Davis and his Battalion were not in Somalia either time longer than "90 days." The rationale of this policy contrasts sharply with the issuance of Bronze Stars and other valor and meritorious service medals to veterans of the Persian Gulf, who were in Saudi Arabia, Kuwait, and Iraq for far less time and under infinitely better conditions than were the 43rd Engineers in Somalia during either deployment.

CHRONOLOGY OF EVENTS

OPERATIONS RESTORE AND CONTINUE HOPE
SOMALIA, EAST AFRICA (1992-1994)

<1992>

December 4, 1992: President Bush ordered U.S. troops to Somalia based on the authority of UN Security Council Resolution 794 which authorized the use of military force by member states to protect the delivery of food relief to an estimated two million starving Somali people. A Pakistani infantry battalion which had already been deployed, exchanged gunfire with Somali gunmen at Mogadishu's airport.

December 9, 1992: Navy Seals and U.S. Marines landed on the coastline at Mogadishu, secured the airport, seaport and former U.S. embassy. Marines and French Foreign Legionnaires seized the weapons from Somali gunmen and secured critical intersections. The first UN World Food Program supply plane landed at Mogadishu's airport.

December 10, 1992: Two Somalis were killed when their "technical" tried to run a French Foreign Legion roadblock. U.S. Marines discovered an arms cache near the U.S. Embassy.

December 11, 1992: U.S. Army engineers and troops landed at a former Soviet air base at Bale Dogle, seventy miles from

210

Mogadishu, to prepare the runway for transports. Food began arriving by plane and sea at Mogadishu.

December 12, 1993: Three Somali "technicals" were destroyed by Marine helicopters when the Marines were fired upon.

December 13, 1993: A reinforced company consisting of 230 Marines landed at Bale Dogle and secured its perimeter. Three hours later, elements of the U.S. Army's 10th Mountain Infantry Division (Light) landed at Bale Dogle.

December 14, 1992: UN Secretary General Boutros-Ghali said that "systematic disarmament of somali's clan militias is a prerequisite to a successful UN peacekeeping operation after U.S. forces depart." A White House official replied, "Disarmament was not a stated part of our mission and that has not changed."

December 24, 1992: Lawrence L. Freeman, 51, U.S. State Department civilian employee, became the first American killed in Somalia when his truck hit a land mine.

January 7, 1993: U.S. Marines raided a fortified arsenal of Somali warlord General Mohammed Farah Aidid after they were fired upon by Somali snipers.

January 8, 1993: Leaders of fourteen Somali factions called for a ceasefire and agreed to hold a national reconciliation conference in Addis Ababa.

Doorway to Hell

<u>January 11, 1993</u>: While Marines raided Mogadishu's arms market and seized a major cache of weapons and ammunition, the Advance Party of the 43rd Engineer Combat Battalion (Heavy) arrived at Mogadishu's airport. The main body arrived soon afterward.

<u>January 12, 1993</u>: PFC Domingo Arroyo, 21, of Elizabeth, New Jersey, United States Marine Corps, was the first of what would become forty three U.S. military casualties, when he was killed in a firefight near the airport.

<u>January 18, 1993</u>: The first reduction of U.S. forces occurred when 850 Marines left Mogadishu. They were replaced by the 900 members of the Australian light infantry regiment.

<u>January 25, 1993</u>: U.S. helicopter gunships backing Belgian paratroopers battled guerrillas outside Kismayu.

<u>February 4, 1993</u>: UN military commanders issued a letter to fourteen Somali political factions requesting that they "list their weapons and supplies by February 15 to expedite the disarmament process."

<u>February 15, 1993</u>: Somalia's warlords failed to meet the UN deadline to turn in a list of their arms inventories.

<u>February 20, 1993</u>: U.S. special envoy Robert Oakley accused the United Nations of stalling its takeover of peacekeeping forces in Somalia. He also accused Turkish LTG Cevik Bir, the newly-appointed commander of UN forces of delaying his arrival and of postponing the transition from "U.S. to UN command."

Doorway to Hell

February 22, 1993: Fighting erupted in Kismayu resulting in the deaths of twenty four Somalis. The fighting postponed the withdrawal of U.S. forces who were scheduled to hand over control of the city to Belgian paratroopers.

February 24, 1993: Supporters of General Mohammed Farah Aidid stoned U.S. and UN forces in Mogadishu, attacked and looted the Egyptian and French embassies, burned tires, and set up roadblocks on the city's main roads. The roadblocks were eventually broken up by U.S. Marines and French Foreign Legionnaires.

March 2, 1993: Robert Oakley declared that the U.S. mission had "largely been accomplished."

March 3, 1993: UN Secretary General Boutros Boutros-Ghali recommended to the Security Council that it create a UN peacekeeping force of 28,000 troops by May 1. The new force was proposed to consist of 20,000 regular troops and 8,000 logistical troops, most of whom would initially be supplied by the U.S.

March 12, 1993: The 43rd Engineer Combat Battalion (Heavy) returned to Fort Benning, Georgia from Somalia, via Djibouti; Cairo, Egypt; Rome, Italy; Shannon, Ireland; and Gander, Newfoundland, Canada.

March 16, 1993: A battle erupted in Kismayu between warring clans., Belgian paratroopers attempted to break it up but were forced to withdraw because one clan used women for shields.

March 18, 1993: The U.S. sent a battalion backed up by warships, jets, and helicopters in a show of force to convince the factions to cease fighting.

March 26, 1993: The UN Security Council passed Resolution 14, setting up a multinational UN peacekeeping force in Somalia (UNOSOM II).

March 28, 1993: Somali faction leaders signed an agreement at Addis Ababa, Ethiopia, to establish an interim government within ninety days.

April 5, 1993: General Colin L. Powell, Chairman of the Joint Chiefs of Staff, declined to set a withdrawal date for U.S. troops, during a visit to Mogadishu.

April 20, 1993: The German government announced commitment of approximately 1,600 troops to Somalia at the request of the UN Secretary General. This would represent the first commitment of German troops outside of Germany since the end of World War II.

May 3, 1993: Approximately 340 U.S. Marines and Army infantrymen left Somalia.

May 4, 1993: LTG Cevik Bir of the Turkish Army assumed command of the UN military operation in Somalia. The multinational forces were projected to reach 28,000 troops including 4,000 Americans. This was the first time that American troops were handed over to a foreign military commander under the category of "operational control."

Doorway to Hell

<u>June 5, 1993:</u> General Mohammed Farah Aidid, wishing to disrupt the progress of the UN which potentially would deprive him of dominating Somalia, unleashed his forces. In the ensuing battle, twenty-four Pakistani soldiers were killed, and fifty-seven UN peacekeeping soldiers were wounded. An additional fifty-four Pakistanis and three Americans were wounded. Mogadishu hospitals reported fifteen Somalis killed and more than one hundred wounded in the fighting.

<u>June 6, 1993:</u> Retired U.S. Admiral Jonathon Howe, Deputy to Boutros-Ghali plastered Mogadishu with posters offering $25,000 reward for the capture of Mohammed Aidid.

<u>June 12, 1993:</u> U.S. planes and ground forces conducted assaults on five targets in Mogadishu.

<u>June 13, 1993:</u> Pakistani soldiers fired on several thousand unarmed Somali demonstrators protesting the U.S. air attacks against warlord General Aidid.

<u>June 17, 1993:</u> After six hours of bombardment and street battles between Aidid's supporters and UN peacekeeping forces, UN troops captured Aidid's headquarters, but Aidid and his aides escaped. The fighting left five UN and sixty Somalis dead, and more than forty-four UN troops and one hundred Somalis wounded.

<u>July 12, 1993:</u> U.S. forces attacked Aidid's stronghold in Mogadishu killing at least fifteen Somalis. Shortly after the attack, mobs of Somalis shot, beat and stoned to death three foreign news photographers.

Doorway to Hell

<u>August 8, 1993</u>: Four American soldiers were killed in Mogadishu by a remote-controlled bomb.

<u>August 18, 1993</u>: According to the State Department, the Sudan supplied military aid to Aidid.

<u>August 22, 1993</u>: A wire-controlled bomb exploded under a HUMVEE, wounding six American soldiers.

<u>August 23, 1993</u>: Les Aspin, Secretary of Defense ordered four hundred U.S. Army Rangers and Delta Force personnel to Somalia.

<u>August 30, 1993</u>: Army Rangers stormed houses suspected of being used by Aidid guerrillas, finding evidence that they had been used by Aidid's gunmen.

<u>September 5, 1993</u>: Seven Nigerian troops were killed in a firefight at a roadblock while attempting to assume control of the roadblock from Italian forces. Italy rejected charges that their troops failed to come to the aid of the Nigerians when they came under fire from Somali snipers.

<u>September 7, 1993</u>: U.S. Army Rangers captured seventeen suspected Aidid guerrillas at a Mogadishu villa after a brief firefight.

<u>September 9, 1993</u>: Somali gunmen clashed with UN forces in Mogadishu. One Pakistani soldier was killed, two Pakistanis and three Americans were wounded. At least sixty Somali gunmen and civilians were killed in the battle.

Doorway to Hell

September 21, 1993: U.S. Army Rangers arrested Osman Ato, the chief financial supporter of Mohammed Farah Aidid during a brief firefight.

September 22, 1993: The UN Security Council adopted Resolution 865 setting March 1995 as the date for ending all UN peacekeeping in Somalia and handing over responsibility for the country to an elected government.

September 25, 1993: Three American soldiers died when their helicopter was shot down in Mogadishu by Somali militia. Three Americans and three Pakistanis were wounded.

October 3-4, 1993: In a battle in the middle of Aidid-controlled territory, one hundred Rangers captured twenty-four of Aidid's supporters. Three Blackhawk helicopters were shot down, eighteen Americans were killed, seventy-five wounded and one American pilot (CW/4 Michael Durant) was captured. The Rangers were pinned down for fifteen hours before reinforcements arrived in the form of Pakistani and Malaysian tanks and armored personnel carriers supported by U.S. Army light infantry.

October 6, 1993: Aidid made an offer to trade CW/4 Michael Durant for Osman Ato.

October 7, 1993: During a televised address to the nation, President Clinton announced that he was ordering an additional 5,300 U.S. troops to Somalia, to include 1,700 combat soldiers and 3,600 Marines. In the same speech, he declared that all U.S. forces would be withdrawn from Somalia not later than March 31, 1994.

October 8, 1993: LTC Robert L. Davis, 43rd Engineer Combat Battalion (Heavy), Fort Benning, Georgia, received a deployment order to return the 43rd to Somalia to build a base camp near Mogadishu for the purpose of housing the U.S. armored task force.

October 9, 1993: Mohammed Farah Aidid offered a ceasefire between U.S. forces and his forces.

October 10, 1993: Secretary of State Warren Christopher declared on NBC's "Meet The Press" that the administration had made mistakes with regard to its Somalia policy and tilted too far toward military action at the expense of diplomacy.

October 13, 1993: President Clinton sent a report to Congress stating that he was sending an additional 3,000 Army combat personnel and 3,600 additional Marines to Somalia.

October 14, 1993: Mohammed Farah Aidid released U.S. helicopter pilot Michael Durant and a Nigerian soldier, Umar Shantali, captured several weeks earlier.

October 16, 1993: President Clinton criticized former President Bush for the initial commitment to Somalia and unleashed a partisan rainstorm of protest and attacks for his delegation of foreign policy.

October 18, 1993: Advance elements of the 43rd Engineer Combat Battalion (Heavy) arrived again at Mogadishu airport, becoming the only battalion-size organization of any service deployed twice to Somalia. Vehicles were issued UNOSOM passes with expiration dates of December 31.

Doorway to Hell

October 28, 1993: Somali gunmen opened fire on Hunter Base near Mogadishu. No U.S. personnel were hit. At the same time Aidid declared Boutros Boutros-Ghali as an individual who "can no longer be regarded as a neutral force."

October 31, 1993: Aidid's position was upheld by other Somali clans. At a UN-sponsored peace conference, of fifteen factions invited, only two showed up.

November 8, 1993: With the Clinton administration under increasing criticism for its Somalia policy, Deputy Secretary of State Clifton Wharton submitted his resignation. He was widely viewed as a sacrificial goat since his duties had little to do with Somalia. At the same time, the Somali security chief for CARE (an international relief agency) was killed in a firefight between Somali gunmen and Malaysian troops in an Aidid stronghold.

December 7, 1993: President Clinton was forced to explain at a press conference why a U.S. plane was used to carry Aidid to a peace conference at Addis Ababa, Ethiopia. His explanation was in response to the furor that was building in the United States against his Somalia policy.

November 14, 1993: An American civilian, Kai Lincoln, 23, New York, working for the United Nations, was shot and killed in a carjacking in Mogadishu.

November 15, 1993: Bandits held up a truck convoy and shot to death fifteen Somalis and wounded thirteen more before escaping with ten of the trucks. Italian troops gave chase and recovered four trucks and handed over four of the bandits to the fledgling Mogadishu Police Force.

November 16, 1993: The UN Security Council voted unanimously to call off the hunt for Mohammed Aidid and lifted the reward that was offered for his capture.

November 18, 1993: Mohammed Aidid emerged from hiding in Mogadishu in triumph and was hailed as a hero by Somalis in Mogadishu.

December 7, 1993: President Clinton was forced to explain to the press why a U.S. plane was used to ferry Aidid to a peace conference at Addis Ababa, Ethiopia, in reaction to a furor from veterans' organizations throughout the United States.

December 15, 1993: Secretary of Defense Les Aspin submitted his resignation for "personal reasons." It was widely speculated in Washington and among the media that Aspin had to be sacrificed because President Clinton was being pummeled over his Somalia policy and his ratings in the polls were dropping to a new low of 37 percent.

December 18, 1993: The 43rd Engineer Combat Battalion (Heavy) loaded aboard a chartered 747 for its flight home, via Cairo, Egypt; Rome, Italy; Paris, France and then to Atlanta, Georgia, from where they would be bused to Fort Benning.

December 19, 1993: The 43rd Engineer Combat Battalion (Heavy) arrived at Fort Benning, Georgia, from Somalia, for the second time.

Doorway to Hell

December 24, 1993: The Pentagon announced that it refused to release the videotape of the Ranger battle on "No-Name Street" on October 3, allegedly because the U.S. troops were using "secret" equipment. This explanation was widely criticized as a "cover story" to prevent the American public from forcing a reluctant administration to reclassify Somalia as a combat zone. (The videotape of the Ranger Raid at the Olympic Hotel in downtown Mogadishu was also classified. It was an open secret in Washington that the classification was to prevent political embarrassment to the administration due to the disastrous outcome.)

January 24, 1994: Somalian gunmen raided a UN World Food Program warehouse in Baidoa, killing one Somali guard and wounding another. On the same day, the UN warned all Somalian warlords that they "had to get their house in order or all aid would be cut."

February 1, 1994: U.S. Marines were attacked while in a truck convoy and killed eight Somalis in an ensuing firefight. Somalis demonstrated, shouting anti-American slogans as they rampaged through the streets of Mogadishu.

February 8, 1994: Major General Thomas R. Montgomery, Commander of all U.S. troops and Deputy Commander of the UN forces left Somalia, leaving approximately 5,000 U.S. troops still in-country and aboard naval vessels off the Somalian coast.

March 18, 1994: Somali gunmen began appearing in force in Kismayu, Baidoa, Bardera, and Mogadishu, traveling in

Technicals and heavily armed. Raids and shooting occurred throughout the day and night in the capital.

March 21, 1994: Two Italian television journalists were gunned down near the Italian embassy in Mogadishu by Somali gunmen who ambushed their vehicle.

March 25, 1994: The last American troops departed from Somalia.

March 30, 1994: A cholera epidemic that began in the northern part of Somalia spread to Mogadishu. At least 3,500 Somalis came down with the disease. Somalis in Mogadishu running radio stations, religious leaders, and editors of newsletters refused to publicize the information needed to avoid cholera without payment from the UN.

April 3, 1994: All warehouses in the new port area of Mogadishu were raided and looted by Somali gunmen. Egyptian guards watched as the Somali looters carried off the contents.

April 7, 1994: Somali warlord Mohammed Farah Aidid appeared at the Pan-African Congress in Kampala, Uganda and addressed the seven hundred delegates, demanding the UN pay reparations for what he claimed to be 13,000 Somalis who were killed during the peacekeeping mission.

May 1, 1994: A bill, co-sponsored by Congressmen Ike Skelton (D-MO) and Mel Reynolds (D-IL) was placed on the calendar of the House Ways and Means Committee that would provide tax exemption for pay, tax filing extensions, home sales tax extension, and death benefits to the service members and families of Somalia veterans.

May 5, 1994: Stung over criticism of the Somalia operation and losses suffered there, Clinton announced Presidential Decision Directive 25 constituting new guidelines on multinational peace operations in the future. He stated that the U.S. would not commit troops in "multinational operations unless they are well-organized, well-planned and in the national interest of the United States." Clarifying the new policy, he implied to questions asked by Congress that U.S. forces would not be assigned to a standing UN army to impose peace, vanquish poverty, or install democracy around the world. However, PDD 25 remained highly classified with the majority of text not made available to the public or to Congress. Eventually, information leaked that PDD 25 would place American troops under U.N. commanders and would even mix foreign troops into U.S. units when called upon to do so. When asked about this, White House spokesmen replied either vaguely or with "no comment."

May 9, 1994: The U.S. Army hosted the Somalia After Action Review Committee at the Army Peacekeeping Institute, U.S. Army War College, Carlisle Barracks, Pennsylvania. The Committee became known as "The Montgomery Board" after the chairman, MG Thomas Montgomery, the senior U.S. commander in Somalia from March, 1993 to March, 1994. Invited to participate were seventy-three flag and field-grade officers, including high ranking civil servants in the Department of Defense, representatives of other services and the Joint Chiefs of Staff.

Doorway to Hell

<u>May 12, 1994:</u> President Clinton presented two posthumous Medals of Honor to the families of two Delta Force NCOs who lost their lives attempting to rescue downed pilot CW4 Michael Durant.

<u>May 13, 1994</u>: After being ignored since October, 1993, families of soldiers killed in the Ranger raid in Mogadishu were invited to the White House to meet with the President, coincidentally only after Democrat Senators on the Committee notified the White House that the families intended to testify against Clinton's foreign policy. When the families emerged from the meeting, several members held a press conference and openly criticized Clinton for "not knowing what was going on in Somalia.

<u>May 14, 1994</u>: The families appeared before the Senate Armed Services Committee and openly questioned a U.S. foreign policy that "is developed haphazardly and implemented by amateurs." At the same hearings, MG Thomas Montgomery, Senior US military commander in Somalia, and MG William Garrison, commander of Somalian special operations, both testified that had U.S. forces had the tanks requested in early September and denied by former Secretary of Defense Les Aspin, they "could have prevented casualties." Additionally, both Generals testified that the U.S. forces did not have the support of AC-130 "Specter" gunships that had been previously withdrawn on Aspin's order. Garrison said, "The Somalis were petrified of the AC-130's!"

<u>May 16, 1994:</u> Five Nepalese soldiers were killed when they intervened in an inter-clan battle in Mogadishu. A wounded Nepalese soldier taken to a nearby hospital was then

224

kidnapped by Somali militiamen. After being turned over to Mohammed Farah Aidid, he was released.

May 20, 1994: Stung over mounting criticism from the press and Congress over an indecisive and confusing foreign policy, and faced with hostile questions regarding his "policy" with regard to Bosnia, Haiti, and North Korea, Clinton "angrily" launched into a lengthy discourse about the achievements of his administration with regard to Russia and the former Soviet republics. While Clinton was defending attacks on his foreign policy, Mohammed Farah Aidid returned in triumph to Mogadishu from Nairobi, Kenya. He thanked thousands of his cheering supporters for defending Somalia against "foreign aggressors."

May 21, 1994: "The Montgomery Board" adjourned and prepared a report to be delivered to Secretary of Defense William Perry containing an analysis of lessons learned. To avoid conflicts with policies above Army level, the recommendations were framed as "observations."

May 23, 1994: Despite the fact that the awards had been recommended and forwarded to the President shortly after the Ranger raid in early October, 1993, President Clinton finally awarded posthumous Medals of Honor to the surviving families of MSG Gary I. Gordon, Lincoln, Maine, and SFC Randall D. Shughart, Newville, Pennsylvania, for their heroism in attempting to rescue CW4 Michael Durant. He did so only after he was informed by Democrat Senators that family members were scheduled to criticize the administration's Somalia policies before Congressional committees. He apparently thought the medals would 'buy them off.' The families testified anyway. These were the first Medals of Honor awarded since the Vietnam War.

May 31, 1994: The United Nations Security Council extended the UN mission in Somalia for another four months instead of six, reflecting the world body's annoyance with the feuding Somali factions.

June 13, 1994: The *Army Times* editorialized that Somalia was worse off than it was prior to the invasion and that no end was in sight. More than 19,000 Third-World country troops remained in Somalia, lacking night vision and aviation assets fielded by the U.S. forces. Stretched thinly across the country, they were incapable of decisive intervention between warring clans.

June 20, 1994: Aidid's forces marched into the city of Marka on the coast south of Mogadishu and simultaneously occupied Beledweyne near the Ethiopian border. More than four thousand U.S. Navy and Marine Corps personnel on ships offshore prepared for the total evacuation of all U.S. diplomats.

June 29, 1994: The U.S. State Department ordered the withdrawal of all American diplomats and support staff from Somalia, transferring the Somalia offices to neighboring Kenya due to a total collapse of security within Mogadishu.

September 1, 1994: The small remaining detachment of State Department personnel maintaining the U.S. diplomatic mission in Somalia lowered the U.S. flag over the former American embassy and evacuated the last American presence from the country. Following the U.S. action, the U.N. Security Council voted to withdraw all remaining U.N. forces from Somalia by January l, 1995.

ENDNOTES

1. HUMINT is the military acronym for HUMan INTelligence, one form of military intelligence which is rarely if ever acted upon without confirmation from other sources.

2. Mohammed Aidid, the leading warlord among four principal warlords in Somalia, had been the Commanding General of the Army of Somalia prior to the revolution in 1990 that plunged the country into chaos.

3. Despite the fact that Delta Force personnel captured Osman Ato, later participated in the Ranger raid at the Olympic Hotel and two members of that force were presented posthumous Medals of Honor, it remained the official position of the U.S. government that no Delta Force Personnel.

4. Diego Garcia is a small island in the middle of the Indian Ocean controlled by the British. Through agreements between Great Britain and the United States, U.S. military forces are permitted access to the island's port and air facilities.

5. "Technicals" was the Somali term for any type of Somali-owned vehicle that was mounted with weaponry. In most instances, they were trucks of one sort or another with Soviet-built machine guns welded to the roof or floor.

6. The Red Crescent Society is the Muslim world's equivalent of the American Red Cross.

7. Due to the disruption of Somalian society, the lexicography of the language has been so disrupted that precise spellings of names and locations vary depending upon sources. For example, one town can have four or five different spellings depending upon the source (eg: Oddur, Xoddur, Odoore, Xodure, etc.)

8. Although the Army sent a team to Fort Drum, New York to counsel with the returning veterans of the 10th Mountain Division (LT), troops who were assigned to other posts in smaller units were not provided the same psychological counseling. An example of this oversight, or lack of counseling resources, was that of the 43d Engineers. Stationed at Fort Benning, since they were a separate battalion attached to the 10th Mountain Division (LT) in Somalia, they were left to recover on their own. The result was that the battalion experienced three times the divorce rate of any other battalion at Fort Benning.

9. Sergeant First Class Osieo Lopez was one of almost 100 personnel transferred from other units within the United States to the 43rd prior to its departure from Fort Benning. In Lopez's case, he was transferred from his home unit at Fort Hood, Texas because the 43rd didn't have a qualified Battalion Communications Chief.

10. Travel near the Ethiopian border was especially dangerous. Due to the Ogaden war between Somalia and Ethiopia, the border of Somalia near Ethiopia contained an

estimated 400,000 Soviet-made anti-personnel and anti-tank land mines that were unrecorded.

11. MREs (Meals Ready to Eat) were the successor to the former "C" Ration issued to veterans of the Korean and Vietnam Wars. Members of the U.S. armed forces who ate them referred to them as "Rees." They also claimed that the initials actually stood for "Meals Rejected by Ethiopians" and "Meals Refusing to Exit" which reflected the impact the highly concentrated food had on the digestive system.

12. This quote was taken from a letter sent home by an NCO with the 3d Battalion, 14th Infantry and was used to frankly describe the elite of the Belgian Army they encountered in Kismayu. He wrote that the Americans looked upon the Belgians as little more than uniformed rabble whose attitudes about the Somalis were "racist" and who regarded the Somalis as only one level higher than the monkeys they were shooting.

13. Mail which was authorized to be sent to "Any Soldier" in the Persian Gulf Theater of Operations during the Persian Gulf War, was discouraged by Department of Defense authorities for those in Somalia because of the lack of postal handling facilities.

14. The heat in Somalia was so intense that unless the soldiers removed the film in their cameras and sent them home for developing as soon as possible, the film would discolor into a red, orange tint.

15. Somalian cockroaches were commonly three to four inches long.

16. Before Australian showers could be set up, the only way to remain reasonably clean in the germ-laden and filthy environment was for the soldiers to wash themselves out of a bucket of water.

17. Anthony Varga was later discharged and became a private contractor for the Army.

18. The $166 million figure was reduced from $253 million that had been requested earlier, a figure at which donor nations balked.

19. It should be noted that Warren Christopher is a member of the Council on Foreign Relations, the driving force behind the formation of the United Nations in 1946.

20. A senior Clinton administration official confirmed that U.S. troops operated under the guidelines of the UN mandate. When asked whether the administration was comfortable with a situation in which Aidid could order his troops to kill U.S. troops, but U.S. soldiers were not allowed to kill Aidid, the official replied, "I don't think I'm going to answer that in terms of the question you asked." Major David Stockwell, UN military spokesman in Mogadishu confirmed the policy in saying, "The mission is to detain him, not kill him. Purposely killing him is contrary to the mission we've been given. If an Army sniper shot him and knew it was Aidid, he would be disobeying orders. If he (Aidid) ends up being killed in a firefight...then that's just the cost of doing business."

21. Without comment MG Guy LaBoa, commander of Fort Carson, Colorado reversed the conviction of Specialist Fourth

Class James Mowris. Base commanders are empowered to reject a court-martial decision if they find legal errors or if they decide a rejection "best serves military justice, discipline or the goal of the mission." Without comment on his decision, there is no record as to why LaBoa reversed the decision. LaBoa was returned to duty with the 984th MP Company without demotion or fine.

22. The military should have by this time recognized that "lessons leared in Vietnam" applied. The Somalis were moving into the guerrilla phase of being supplied in quantity by outside sources, similar to the Vietcong being supplied from North Vietnam by way of the Ho Chi Minh Trail.

23. Somali guerrillas were under no obligation to treat prisoners under the provisions of the Geneva Convention. Neither the UN force in Somalia or the Somalian militia were subject to the governing articles of the Geneva Convention since neither represented a state, according to UN spokesman Fred Eckhart. Although the UN maintained that it would be guided by the Geneva Conventions in the treatment of Somali prisoners it detained, neither Aidid or any other Somali warlord had any obligation to do the same.

24. Count Carl Von Clausewitz, *On War* (Princeton, New Jersey: Princeton University Press, 1984), 606.

25. Congressman James Inhofe (R-Okla) who represented the lst Congressional District of Oklahoma was elected in November, 1994 as the Junior United States Senator from Oklahoma.

26. Task Force 1/64 was formed around the 1st Battalion, 64th Armored battalion from Fort Stewart, Georgia.

27. Where Department of Defense regulations prohibit any extra payment to American military personnel, the prohibition doesn't apply to civilians. One hundred civilian employees from the Army Material Command in Alexandria, Virginia were sent to Somalia. They received 25 percent added to their base pay as a hardship allowance and another 25 percent as danger pay. Mark Walter, a GS-9 electronics technician from Tobyhanna Army Depot, Pennsylvania who had been deployed to Saudi Arabia confirmed the opinion of military veterans of both theaters of operation when he said, "Somali was far more dangerous than Saudi Arabia."

28. In comparison, during the Vietnam war the troops were awarded two medals: the Vietnam Service Medal (by the U.S. Government), and the Vietnam Campaign Medal (by the Vietnamese Government). In addition, those who landed prior to August, 1965, were awarded the Armed Forces Expeditionary Medal as were those in Somalia.

29. Other combat-recognized awards were also issued including the Combat Infantryman's Badge to members of the 10th U.S. Mountain Division (L).

30. In one instance, a National Guard infantry Captain who volunteered for active duty for the Persian Gulf War received the Bronze Star in spite of the fact that he arrived in Riyadh on the last day of the ground war and remained in Riyadh.

31. When TF-164 was transported from Fort Stewart, Georgia its M-1 Abrams tanks were flown to Somalia by C5-A Galaxy transport planes, the only planes in the American inventory that could airlift the Abrams tank. Eighteen C5-A Galaxy transports were committed by the Air Force to airlift the entire Task Force from Hunter Army Airfield in Savannah, Georgia.

32. Hackworth is a highly decorated veteran and author of numerous books and articles on various military subjects, following his retirement from the Army after a distinguished career.

33. Dellums was Chairman of the House Armed Services Committee, member of the Black Caucus and a former anti-war demonstrator during Vietnam.

34. The reluctance of Americans to allow their troops to be placed under command of foreign leaders was more than three quarters of a century long. When U.S. Army General John J. "Black Jack" Pershing was informed by Field Marshal Ferdinand Foch that his troops would be fed into depleted French units in 1917, Pershing denied the concept and insisted they remain under American command. President Wilson supported Pershing and foch was forced to back down.

35. Colonel Kenneth Allard, a senior Fellow at the Institute for National Strategic Studies, Washington D.C. was commissioned by the Joint Chiefs of Staff to conduct a study of the Somalian operation. In a publication entitled Somalia Operations: Lessons Learned (National Defense University Press, Washington D.C.) 1995, he concluded that the U.S. forces were subjected to a convoluted command system set up

by the U.S. military in the latter stages of the Somalia operation that undercut the unity of command principle.

35. UCMJ - Uniform Code of Military Justice, that by U.S. statute serves as a separate code of law for U.S. military personnel apart from civil or criminal law in any other jurisdiction.

36. President Clinton, as a student wrote a letter to a former instructor thanking him for helping him avoid induction. He used the word "loathed" when addressing the subject of his view of the armed forces. During the Presidential campaign, extraordinary efforts were made by the Clinton campaign staff to destroy all copies of that letter. However, the original recipient kept a copy and it surfaced after Clinton was elected.

38. Most Americans do not realize that those selected to attend Oxford on the Rhodes Scholarship have been hand-picked to be molded into what Cecil Rhodes envisioned when he started the scholarship program: globalists. By funding the program, Rhodes, who, along with other European monarchists and landed families, ensured that his vision for the future--a deletion of individual nation-states, replaced by a socialist one-world government--would grow and prosper. Clinton was a product of this program.

Bibliography

Primary Sources:

Bochonok, Captain Jeffrey T., S-l (Personnel/Admin Officer) - 43rd Engineer Combat Battalion (Heavy), Operation Continue Hope. Telephone interview by author, April 13, 1994.

Command Relationships (Operation Continue Hope), FORSCOM Operations Center, Command Diagram IS-DSN, U.S. Army, 15 October 1993.

Davis, Lieutenant Colonel Robert L., Commander, 43rd Engineer Combat Battalion (Heavy), Operations Restore and Continue Hope. Interview by author, December 23, 1993, Fort Benning, Georgia.

Dodson, Mrs. Gia, Corporate Headquarters, Phillips Petroleum Company. Interview by author, April 14, 1994, Bartlesville, Oklahoma.

Estes, Major Allen C., S-3 (Operations Officer), 43rd Engineer Combat Battalion (Heavy), Operation Restore Hope. Telephone interview, by author, April 4, 1994.

Feierstein, Major Mark, S4 (Logistics Officer) - 36th Engineer Group, Operation Restore Hope; S3 (Operations Officer) - 43rd Engineer Combat Battalion (Heavy), Operation Continue Hope. Interview by author, December 23, 1993, Fort Benning,

Georgia. Telephone interviews by author, March 4, 25, 27, and 31, 1994.

Forrester, Captain Dale, Chaplain - 43rd Engineer Combat Battalion (Heavy), Operation Restore Hope. Telephone interview by author, March 31, 1994.

3rd Engineer Combat Battalion (Heavy) FRAGOs (Fragmentary Orders) to OPORD 93-2 (Continue Hope), Mogadishu, Somalia (160 Documents). Date Groups: 18 November 1993 - 16 December 1993.

SITREPS (Situation Reports), Commander-Falcon Brigade, Embassy Compound, Mogadishu, Somalia (48 Documents). Date/Time Groups: 280900OCT93 to 161600DEC93.

OPORD (Operation Order) 93-2 (Operation Continue Hope), Mogadishu, Somalia. November 13, 1993 (One document with attached annexes).

Hagberg, Mrs. Wanda, Executive Secretary to the Commander, 36th Engineer Group Headquarters. Telephone interview by author, March 29, 1994.

Inhofe, Hon. James M., (R-lst District, Oklahoma), Letter to Mr. and Mrs. Don Boyer, Tulsa, Oklahoma. (On November 8, 1994, Congressman Inhofe was elected as the Junior United States Senator from Oklahoma)

Maxwell, Command Sergeant Major Lawrence, CSM-43rd Engineer Combat Battalion (Heavy), Operations Restore

Hope and Continue Hope. Telephone interview by author, March 28, 1994.

Smith, Sergeant Hans, Operations NCO - HSC, 43rd Engineer Combat Battalion (Heavy); Somalian Aid Mission, 1985, and Operation Continue Hope. Telephone interview by author, March 4, 1994.

United States Department of Defense, Map, <u>Muqdishu</u>, Series Y921, Edition 6-DMA, Sheet 1, Defense Mapping Agency, Hydrographic/Topographic Agency, Bathesda, Maryland.

United States Library of Congress: U.S. Senate Joint Resolution 45, 103rd U.S. Congress, February 4, 1993. U.S. House of Representatives Joint Resolution 173, 103rd U.S. Congress, May 25, 1993.

Wheeler, 1LT Brian E., Signal Officer - 43rd Engineer Combat Battalion (Heavy), Operations Restore Hope and Continue Hope. Interviews by author, May 15 and December 28, 1993, Fort Benning, Georgia. Telephone interviews by author, March 17, 24, and 31, 1994. Letters, Somalia to author, Tulsa, November 3, 1993, and February 28, 1994.

Newspapers and Periodicals:

Associated Press News Service Stories (Chronological Order):

"Congressman speaks out against U.S. intervention in Somalia." *Columbus* (GA) *Ledger-Enquirer*, December 3, 1992, B-6.

"Clinton Backs Bush's Decision on Somalia." *Tulsa World*, December 4, 1992, A-1.

"U.N. Forces Going To Somalia." *Tulsa World*, December 5, 1992, A-1.

"U.N. Chief Optimistic On Somalia." *Tulsa World*, December 6, 1992, A-16.

"Military Readying More Support Troops For Deployment." *Tulsa World*, December 6, 1992, A-16.

"U.S. Warjets Scout Somalia." *Tulsa World*, December 8, 1992, A-3.

"Gun Prices Decline On Eve of Marine's Landing." *Tulsa World*, December 9, 1992, A-2.

"U.S. Troops Land In Somalia." *Tulsa World*, December 9, 1992, A-1.

"2 Somalis Killed At Checkpoint." *Tulsa World*, December 11, 1992, A-2.

"Marines Make First Food Run." *Tulsa World*, December 13, 1992, A-1.

"Experts warn against loss of Somali livestock . . . crops." *Columbus Ledger-Enquirer*, December 22, 1992, A-4.

Doorway to Hell

"Army civilian killed by mine." *Columbus Ledger-Enquirer*, December 24, 1992, A-1.

"Shelling Lights Up Sky In Clan Battle." <u>Meridian (MS) Star</u>, January 1, 1993, A-1.

"Gunmen Attack Aid Group's Compound." *Daytona Beach (FL) News Journal*, January 2, 1994, A-6.

"Somali Sniper Hits 2nd U.S. Casualty." *Daily Oklahoman* (Oklahoma City), January 14, 1993, A-1.

"Troops Find `Mother Lode' of Weapons in Somalia." *Tulsa World*, January 17, 1993, A-1.

"Marine is shot as Several More Troops Return." *Stillwater (OK) News Press*, January 20, 1993, A-1.

"Somalia Pullout Delayed." *Kansas City Star*. January 22, 1993, A-4.

"U.S. Marine Killed In Mogadishu." *Tulsa World*, January 26, 1993, A-1.

"Slain Marine Lauded in Hometown." *Tulsa World*, January 27, 1993, A-11.

"U.N. dragging its feet on Somalia, U.S. envoy says." *Columbus Ledger-Enquirer*, January 28, 1993, B-4.

"2,700 soldiers to leave Somalia." *Kansas City Star*, February 1, 1993, C-1.

240

"U.S. Marines say Somalis mistaken about death of six." *Kansas City Star*, February 6, 1993, A-8.

"Somali clans battle in capital." Dallas Morning News, February 7, 1993, A-l4.

"Coalition armies take wider roles in Somalia." *Kansas City Star*, February 13, 1993, A-1.

"U.N. May Take Over Somalia Command." *Tulsa World*, February 14, 1993, A-2.

"Australian soldiers kill Somali gunmen, wound two others." *Columbus Ledger-Enquirer*, February 18, 1993, A-1.

"Troops Kills Somali Protester." *Tulsa World*, February 19, 1993, A-1.

"Troops Prepare To Exit; Kids Show Weapons." *Saturday Oklahoman and Times* (Oklahoma City), February 20, 1993, A-3.

"U.S. Envoy Warns A Somali Leader." *New York Times*, February 24, 1993, A-22.

"Soldier Killed in Somalia; Marines Face Hearings." *Tulsa Daily World*, March 4, 1993, A-2.

"Marine says he shot Somalis in self defense." *Dallas Morning News*, March 6, 1993, A-10.

"Marines are killing us." *Kansas City Star*, March 7, 1993, A-16.

"U.S. Troops On Alert In Somalia." *Daily Oklahoman* . March 10, 1993, A-3.

"UN seeks aid for Somalia." *Kansas City Star*, March 11, 1993, A-1.

"Disease New Killer In Somalia." *Daytona Beach News Journal*, March 30, 1993, A-1.

"Clinton Orders 400 More U.S. Troops Sent To Somalia." *Daily Oklahoman*, August 24, 1993, A-1.

Christopher Cites Errors On Military Action In Somalia." *Dallas Morning News*, October 11, 1993, A-1.

"Clinton Critical Of UN And Bush On Somalia Campaign." *Columbus Ledger-Enquirer*, October 16, 1993, B-7.

"Gunmen Attack Aid Group's Compound." *Daytona Beach News Journal*, January 2, 1994, A-1.

"Somali Relief Workers Flee As Gunmen Loot Warehouses."

Daytona Beach News Journal, January 30, 1994, A-1.

"Marines Firing In Self-Defense Kill 8, Injure Many, In Somalia." *Daytona Beach News Journal*, February 2, 1994, A-1.

"Cholera Outbreak Spreads In Somalia." *Daytona Beach News Journal*, February 24, 1994, A-2.

"Cholera Outbreak Spreads To Mogadishu." *Daytona Beach News Journal*. February 28, 1994, A-2.

"Battle-Scarred U.S. Brigade Leaves Somalia." *Daytona Beach News Journal*, March 2, 1994, A-1.

"Renewed Civil War Feared After Troops Leave Somalia." *Daytona Beach News Journal*, March 13, 1994, A-1.

"Somalis Abduct American Worker." *Daytona Beach News Journal*, April 1, 1994, A-1.

"Small Arms Market Supplies World's Skirmishes." *Tulsa World*, April 5, 1994, A-6.

"Ill-Fated Somalia Raid Angered Clinton." *Daytona Beach News Journal*, May 13, 1994, A-2.

"Pair Killed In Somalia Due Honors." *Daytona Beach News Journal*. May 15, 1994, A-4.

"President Defends Foreign Policy." *Tulsa World*, May 20, 1994, A-5.

Atkinson, Rick. "Rebuilding Somalia-within the UN compound." *The Washington Post*, weekly edition, March 28-April 3, 1994, 16.

Auster, Bruce B. and Greg Ferguson. "Caught In The Cross-fire." *U.S. News And World Report*, December 6, 1993, 32.

Beauchamp, et al. "Province and Dispersal of Cretaceous Celastics in Northeastern Africa: Climatic and Structural Setting." *Petroleum Abstracts*, 31, no 6, Abstract 496, August, 1991.

Bendel, Mary Ann. "A Sense of Urgency, Uncertainty at 2 bases." *USA Today*, December 4, 1992, A-3.

Beydoun, Z.R. "The Red Sea/Gulf of Aden Hydrocarbon Potential Reassessment." *Petroleum Extracts*, ISS 8, no. 6, Abstract 31, August-1991.

Burns, Christopher, "American dies in Somalia; Marines face shooting hearings." *Daytona Beach News Journal*, March 4, 1993, A-5.

Brown, Mark. "Veteran Newsman Describes Somalia as Hellhole." *Orange County Register*; reprint *Tulsa Daily World*. December 13, 1992, A-13.

Church, George. "They Beat Me Violently With Their Fists And Sticks," *Time*, October 18, 1993, 45.

Claybrook, Clint (Chronological Order):

"1,000 Benning engineers put on alert." *The Benning Leader* (Fort Benning, GA), December 11, 1992, A-4.

"Experts warn against loss of Somali livestock . . . crops." *Columbus Ledger-Enquirer*, December 22, 1992, A-4.

"Oops! Commander wishes troops well in `Bosnia.' *Columbus Ledger-Enquirer*, January 8, 1993, B-1.

"Engineers' road gets marketplace back in business." *Columbus Ledger-Enquirer*, February 4, 1993, A-1.

"Ancient ways clash with modern." *Columbus Ledger-Enquirer*, February 5, 1993, A-5.

"Engineers build roads, comforts." *Columbus Ledger-Enquirer*, February 7, 1993, A-6.

"Supplies hit snags in system," *Columbus Ledger-Enquirer*, February 15, 1993, A-1.

"Notes from Somalia." *Columbus Ledger-Inquirer*, February 20, 1993, A-1.

Copson, Raymond W., *Operation Restore Hope and UNOSOM II*. Foreign Affairs and National Defense Division, Library of Congress, 1993.

Dahlberg, John-Thor. "U.S. Troops Sweep Key City." *New York Times*, January 31, 1993, A-18.

Davis, LTC Robert L. and Major Allen Estes. "Peace-Makers in Somalia." *Engineer*, Submitted copy for pub- lication, March 22, 1993, A-3.

Davis, LTC Robert L. and Major Mark D. Feierstein. "Return To Somalia: The Construction of Victory Base." *Engineer*, Submitted copy for publication, February 17, 1994, A-1.

DeJong, Peter. "U.S. Envoy: Somalia safe for aid deliveries." *Daytona Beach News Journal*, March 3, 1993, A-1.

Department of the Army. "Somalia." Pamphlet 550-86, Department of the Army, 1992.

Donaldson, T. Douglas. "Get Out Of Somalia." *The American Legion.*, January, 1994, 20.

Duffy, Michael, et. al. "How did this happen? Clinton demanded of Les Aspin." *Time*, October 18, 1993, A-49.

Adams, Juanita. *Somalia Background Notes*. Washington D.C.: U.S. Department of State, Bureau of Public Affairs, Office of Public Communications, April, 1986, DN 86-926F.

Birbel, Craig, I. *The Texas Connection: The Assassination of John F. Kennedy*. Scottsdale, AZ: TCC Publishers, 1991.

Branaman, Brenda M., *Somalia: Military Command Arrangements*. Washington D.C.: Foreign Affairs and National Defense Division, Library of Congress, October 15, 1993, 93-93F.

Bruner, Edward F. *Somalia: Military Command Arrangements.*Washington D.C.: Foreign Affairs and National Defense Division, Library of Congress, November 4, 1992, 93-959FO.

Central Intelligence Agency. *Communist Aid Activities To Non-Communist, Less Developed Nations: 1954-1979* (DECLASSIFIED). Washington D.C.: National Foreign Assessment Center, October-1980, ER-80-10318U.

Grimmett, Richard F. *Somalia: Arms Deliveries.* Washington D.C.: Foreign Affairs and National Defense Division, Library of Congress, Document 93-934F, October 28, 1993.

Hackworth, David H. "Spin Doctors Clouding Probe of Bloody Fight." *Army Times,* June 6, 1994.

Hoffman, Marck S. (ed.) *The World Almanac and Book of Facts* - 1993. New York: Scripps Howard & Co., 1993.

Josephy, Alvin M. Jr. (ed.) *World War I.* New York: American Heritage Publishing Co., Inc., 1964.

Kirkpatrick, Jeane. "Clinton's Real Mistake in Somalia." *Reader's Digest,* January, 1994.

Nelson, Harold D. *Somalia: A Country Study.* Washington D.C.: Foreign Area Studies, The American University, 1981.

Roberts, Craig. *Kill Zone: A Sniper Looks at Dealey Plaza.* Tulsa, OK: Consolidated Press Int'l, 1993.

Somalia Fact Sheet. Washington D.C.: Library of Congress, Foreign Affairs and Defense Division, October 18, 1993, 93-9113F.

Shakespeare, William. *The Life of Henry V,* act IV, scene III, Lines
64-67.

Sulzberger, C.L. *World War II.* Arlington, Virginia: American Heritage, 1966.

Sustaining Soldier Health and Performance in Somalia: Guidance For Small Unit Leaders. Fort Detrick, Maryland: U.S. Army Medical Research and Development Command, December 22, 1992.

Toffler, Alvin. *The Third Wave.* New York: William Morrow and Company, 1980.

U.S. State Department. *Somalia: A Country Study.* Washington D.C.: U.S. Government Printing Office, 1992.

Wallace, Robert. *The Italian Campaign,* World War II Series. New York: Time-Life Books, Inc. 1978.

Consulted Sources

U.S. General Accounting Office (Chronological Order):

Africa Watch, "Human Rights Abuses and Civil War in the North: A Report From the U.S. General Accounting Office." New York: 1989.

Somalia: Evading Reality. New York: 1990.

Somalia: A Fight To The Death. New York: 1992.

Somalia: No Mercy In Mogadishu. New York: 1992.

Biles, Peter. "Somalia: Starting from Scratch." *Africa Report*, Vol. 36, No. 3, May-June 1991, 55-59.

Bongartz, Maria. "The Civil War In Somalia: Its Genesis and Dynamics." Upsala, Sweden: Scandinavian Institute of African Affairs, 1991.

Compagnon, Daniel. "The Somali Opposition Fronts: Some Comments and Questions," *Horn of Africa* Vol 13, Nos. 1-2, January-June 1990.

Crozier, Brian. *The Soviet Presence in Somalia*. London: Institute for the Study of Conflict, 1975.

Dagne, Theodore. "Somalia: Current Conditions and U.S. Policy." Washington D.C.: Library of Congress, Report for Congress, 90-252F, May 12, 1990.

Dolley, Margaret. "Somalia: Economy." *Africa South of the Sahara*, 1993.

Earer, Tom J. "War Clouds on the Horn of Africa: A Crisis For Detente." New York: Carnegie Endowment for International Peace, 1976.

Gersony, Robert. "Why Somalis Flee: A Synthesis of Accounts of Conflict Experience in Northern Somalia by Somali Refugees, Displaced Persons, and Others." Washington D.C.: Department of State, 1989.

Greenfield, Richard. "Siad's Sad Legacy." London: *Africa Report*, vol 36, no. 2, March-April 1991.

Gulhati, Ravi. "The Making of Economic Policy in Africa". Washington, World Bank, 1989.

Henze, Paul B. (Chronological Order):

The Horn of Africa: From War To Peace. New York: St. Martin's Press, 1991.

"How Stable Is Siad Barre's Regime." London: *Africa Report*, vol. 27, no. 2, March-April 1992, 54-58.

Lefebvre, Jeffrey A. Arms For The Horn: U.S. Security Policy In Ethiopia and Somalia 1953-1991. Pittsburgh: University of Pittsburgh Press, 1991.

Laitin, David D. *Politics, Language and Thought The Somali Experience*. Chicago: University of Chicago Press, 1977.

Legum, Colin (ed.). "Africa Contemporary Record: Annual Survey and Documents." New York: *Africana*, 1980-1992.

Omaar, Rakiya. "Somalia: At War With Itself." *Current History*, Vol 91, No. 565, May 1992.

Samatar, Ahmed. *Socialist Somalia: Rhetoric and Reality* London: Zed Books, 1988.

Samatar, Said S. (Chronological Order):

"How to Save Somalia." *Washington Post*, December 1, 1992.

In The Shadow Of Conquest: Islam In Colonial Northeast Africa. Trenton: Red Sea Press, 1992.

Spencer, John Hathaway. "The Horn of Africa and U.S. Policy." Cambridge: Institute for Foreign Policy Analysis, 1977.

"Post Report: Somalia." Washington D.C.: U.S. State Department, 1992.

"Somalia: Report on an Amnesty International Visit and Current Human Rights Concerns." London: Amnesty International, 1990.United States Department of State. *Country Reports on Human Rights Practices for 1991.* (Report submitted to 2nd Session, 102nd Congress, House of elations.) Washington D.C., Government Printing Office, February, 1992.

Doorway to Hell

INDEX

MILITARY UNITS

LOCATIONS/ INDIVIDUALS/SUBJECTS